# Just Gill

# Just Gill

## The Story of Gill Dalley, co-founder of Soi Dog Foundation

www.victorinapress.com

Typesetting and Layout: Jorge Vasquez
Photographs courtesy of Soi Dog Foundation
Cover design © Fiona Zechmeister

British Library Cataloguing in Publication Data
A catalogue record for this book is available from the
British Library.
ISBN: 978-1-8380360-1-0 (Paperback)

Typeset in 12pt Garamond
Printed and bound in Great Britain by 4edge ltd.

# Just Gill
Content list

Dedication by John Dalley
Foreword by Donna Freelove (UK President Soi Dog Foundation)
How this book came to be written
Poem by Gill Dalley: You Keep on Walking by … Why, Why, Why?

# Chapter List

# Dedication

*TO GILL*

You are the bravest person I have ever known. That you chose to share the past twenty-five years of your life with me and to love me makes me the luckiest person alive.

If your spirit is out there somewhere, darling, know that I love you and always will.
My only regret of our life together is that I did not let you know how I felt as often as you needed to know it.

If there is one message that I know Gill would like people to get from this book, it is that it does not matter how ordinary you think you are or what difficulties or disabilities come your way – anybody who is determined can make this world a better place and, perhaps more importantly, inspire others to do the same.

**John Dalley, Phuket, Thailand, 2018**

# Foreword by Donna Freelove
## (UK President Soi Dog Foundation)

When Gill and I sat making the original notes for *Just Gill*, there was a Plan A – the story that would be told if her adoptive mother was still alive – and a Plan B – the story that would be told if her adoptive mother had passed away by the time the book was published.

Unfortunately, there was no Plan C.

Why would there have been? Gill had no intention of dying 'while she still had work to do' . . . while the dogs and cats of Asia still needed her. Even on the day that her diagnosis and prognosis was confirmed, she assured me over the phone that she wasn't going to die; it was out of the question.

'I'm not going anywhere, I've fought bigger things than this.'

This was by no means a display of arrogance or Gill thinking that she was indestructible. It was sheer determination; she had a job to do. For whatever reason, and by God knows who, she had been given this relentless task of saving animals and would be sticking around to finish the job.

So there was no contingency for what version was to be told if Gill passed. Certain negatives about her childhood that she may or may not have shared at the time of publishing need, in my opinion, to remain scribbled in note form in my box and heart full of Gill memories, as sadly I am unable to ask her if she still wants them shared or not.

I'm not sure if she would have deleted some of the bad stuff when it actually came to going to print or not. She certainly wanted it 'warts and all' about herself, but she was such a softie that I have to assume she would have opted to edit out anything that would seriously affect anyone but herself.

A couple of things she was adamant about: that the title of her story was to be *Just Gill* and that the cover picture was to be the one which has been used in this book because it is a photo that she felt showed her at her happiest, surrounded by waifs and strays. The cover photo was taken purely by accident by John's sister Karin and had always been a favourite of Gill's, and in my view captures the essence of her.

She also wanted the poem 'You Keep On Walking By, Why, Why, Why?'

to be in the book as she wrote it in the depths of deep despair over a dog and I guess her question of 'why' has never been answered.

Another fact that she wanted to reveal was that her very first connection made with an animal that she wanted to protect from abuse was, in fact, a hamster. That's where her first overwhelming feeling of wanting to save an animal first started. It got her into dreadful trouble with her mother, but the hamster was saved.

Dear, kind Gill . . . all creatures great and small.

The words below are Gill's thoughts when she talked to me about writing her biography, which she wanted to call *Just Gill*. Sadly, the writing of the book was delayed due to Gill's dedication to the building of the animal hospital at the Soi Dog Foundation shelter in Phuket, Thailand.

*I have been approached many times over the years by people asking to write my life story. Each time I've laughed to myself at the absurdity of anyone wanting to read about me. What's so interesting about me, a double amputee? Who on earth would want to read my story? What have I done that anybody else couldn't do?*

*Do you know how many people come up to John and I to tell us how wonderful we are and how 'they couldn't do what we have'? What absolute nonsense!*

*I try to say this as kindly as I can, but nonetheless I do find the notion absurd because John and I are normal people, whatever normal means.*

*We don't consider ourselves to be special, and both of us cringe when others do. We witnessed a problem with stray dogs and tried to help eradicate some of it.*

*We tried to save some wretched souls and everything escalated from there.*

*I'm not saying that we've done everything the right way, we have made mistakes and learned along the way, but always, always the animals came first for us both.*

*The welfare of the animals has been paramount in all of this. We have fought among ourselves about the right way of doing things. Fought and screamed at each other and cried. Every time we disagreed we ultimately came to the same conclusion: that what is in the best interest of the animals is the absolute only way.*

*So when I finally thought that maybe, just maybe, I could write my story in the hope that someone may wish to read it, I decided that I could only do this by sharing my innermost thoughts with a friend, Donna [Freelove].*

*I haven't had the sort of life that I would be comfortable sharing with a stranger. Would they understand? Would they think me mad? I'm certainly not a victim and would never allow myself to succumb to that, but my life before John Dalley (BJD) was not the life that I would bestow on any other woman.*

*I'd been unlucky I guess, but God knows how lucky I've been since I found my soulmate in John and that together we have been able to at least make some inroads into changing* attitudes towards dogs and cats in Asia.

That makes me the richest woman on earth and certainly makes up for a sad life BJD.

Looking back at my early life in simple terms, I was given away as a baby, unwanted, my presence bought shame on my birth mother who had an ultimatum to give me away or lose her marriage.

Of course I've asked myself a thousand times what I did to deserve this. I didn't ask to be born. I didn't ask to be the shameful embarrassment that I clearly was.

I was adopted into a dysfunctional family situation for far from the right reasons. My adoptive mother, another 'pillar of the community' (like my birth mother apparently) bullied me, as well as my wonderfully kind, sensitive and loving but very weak adoptive father.

God, I loved him and he loved me, but he wasn't a strong enough man to stand up to his wife, personally or for me.

Until JD [John Dalley] came into my life, my adopted father was the only human being I ever felt completely loved by. If only he had been a stronger man, for his own self and for me.

It isn't necessary to go into the detail of my harsh upbringing at the hands of my adoptive mother because it doesn't matter now.

Like a desperate child I've tried all my adult life to earn some credit, respect, acknowledgment that I'm a good, honest, hardworking person, that I am respected by most, but not by my adoptive mother.

For example, when I phoned her in excitement from my home in Thailand to tell her that I was going to be on her local Leeds TV news as they are doing a feature on John and my work, she has responded by saying that some guy down the road at number 10 had a promotion at work!

When I lost my legs, my mother's reaction was not to fly out to see me but to ask 'Will you put all this dog nonsense behind you now and come back to the UK?'

She spoke of the Soi Dog Foundation as if it was some sort of a cult. There was no acknowledgment that John and I were dedicating our retirement to saving lives and making a huge difference.

To some this may sound funny, but to the inner child still yearning for some acknowledgment this was very hard and still hurtful.

Why do we put ourselves through things knowing in our heart of hearts that we will be rejected again and again?

I made the huge mistake of contacting my birth mother, again reaching out for some sort of belonging or attachment to an actual family member. Rejected. It was confirmed to me that I'm still the shameful embarrassment that I was the second I was conceived.

Who knows what effect any of these experiences has had on me as a person. I have dealt with bulimia, attempted suicide and felt wretched anger and insecurity at times, but still have an intense pull to help animals, people, anyone who feels unloved and lost in life.

I always want to reach out and make them better.

I feel drawn to the underdog, both animal and human. I feel happiest reaching out and *holding others who stumble around in the wilderness feeling unloved, as I have been there and am surely living proof that anything can be overcome, mentally and physically.*

*Life may never be perfect, but one can make the most of what you have and just deal with what you don't have. There is always, always, someone, somewhere worse off than you and it helps to remember that.*

*I'm imagining that most people who read my story will have a passion for rescuing animals; if I can only get one message over then let it be that you too do make a difference. Whatever part you play, big or small, it is massive to the one soul that is saved or whose pain is lessened because of you.*

*People say that animals don't have a voice. I would always argue that they do have a voice; the trouble is that nobody listens. Please listen to them and act in their best interests at all times.*

*So here I am, 'Just Gill', no more, no less. Dedicating my story to the man who saved me, JD, my eternal love. I could not have achieved what we have with Soi Dog without him or him without me. I have loved this man from the day I met him. He has cared for me in ways that a husband should never need to care for a wife and I don't know whether he realises that it is he who is my world, my strength and my inspiration.*

# How this book came to be written
## by John Dalley

This is an unusual book in that it is written in the first person in autobiographical form by me, Gill's husband. I have written it because I know it is something Gill wanted to do, but, sadly, she died before getting started. Her intention was to write it with her dear friend Donna and to include, in her words, 'warts and all'.

She wanted to call it Just Gill because in her eyes she was just a very ordinary person. However, in my eyes (and I accept that I am biased, but also in the eyes of many thousands of people, many of whom never met Gill) she was an extraordinary person.

As one lady, who I never met but who wrote to me after Gill had died, pointed out: 'Many people see things wrong in this world. Most, though, do nothing, a few determine to actually try and do something about it, very few not only do something about it, but inspire others to do the same.'

Gill was one of the latter group and also overcame severe disabilities in doing so.

Another person wrote, 'I am so sorry for your loss, but how lucky you were to have shared your life with someone so special.'

I do indeed feel lucky to have known and loved her.

If there is one message I know Gill would like people to get from this book, it is that it does not matter how ordinary you feel you are or what difficulties or disabilities come your way – anybody who is determined can make this world a better place.

Since her death, many return volunteers who have met her on previous trips have told me how much in awe they were of her when they first met her or were in her presence.

Gill would have found this ridiculous. She was asked numerous times to share her story, but could not see why anybody would be interested. 'I am just Gill,' she said.

Sadly, her sudden and untimely death in February 2017 meant she ran out of time. As the person who knew her better than anybody, including her 'warts and all', I have therefore taken up the challenge to try to put myself in Gill's shoes and tell her story in what I hope is a way she would be happy with.

# You Keep on Walking By . . . Why, Why, Why?

## A poem by Gill Dalley

*I have been like this for months and you keep walking by.*
*You do not help me you just keep walking by*
*You do not see my hunger or thirst you just keep walking by*
*You do not see my pain you just keep walking by*
*When you do see me all you feel is disgust. Why, Why, Why?*
*I come near you for help you chase me away. Why, Why, Why?*
*My cancer tumours grow as does the pain, you ignore me. Why, Why, Why?*
*You are many humans but show me no humanity. Why, Why, Why?*
*Today my pain has gone as I am taken from this world to the next*
*For the first time in my life I was stroked and kissed as I slipped away*
*Why did I have to wait until my last minutes to feel love? Why, Why, Why?*

# Prologue
# Not all that it seems
## by John Dalley

Looking back, it was that fateful meeting with a stray Soi dog named Naga more than twenty years ago which was to prove life-changing, setting us both off on a testing path of discovery. Although Gill and I didn't realise it at the time, Naga's tragic tale was the catalyst for everything that was to follow, shaping our destiny and leading to challenges neither of us had ever experienced or could have imagined.

We first discovered Thailand when we got married in Phuket on 13 March 1998. We loved the country and the people from the outset; however, what we learned on that first visit was that when it comes to animal welfare in Asia, all is not as it seems.

Gill and I took a month off work and after a few days in Hong Kong flew to Chiang Mai, then Mae Hong Sorn near the Burmese border, on to Bangkok then down to Phuket for our wedding and to the paradise island of Krabi for our honeymoon.

In Phuket after our wedding, we were invited to the hotel's weekly guests' cocktail party in the garden. Here we met a Swiss lady who introduced us to a handsome dog called Naga who was by her side on a lead wearing a bandana around his neck. Obviously this was not just unusual but a unique situation.

I now realise Naga was at least part Bangkaew, which is one of only two recognised Thai breeds – a medium-sized Spitz-type dog.

He had a scab on his head, which the lady told us was the result of a wound he'd had when she came across him in the hotel grounds.

She had taken him to a vet to have the wound treated and also to be vaccinated, before having him bathed and groomed.

Naga certainly looked happy and well and was extremely friendly with anybody who approached him, although he was clearly wary of the Thai waiters who were bringing drinks around.

The hotel's general manager remarked what a lovely dog he was, but I sensed he was not overly happy to see him there.

The lady told us she always spent several weeks in Thailand, but would be returning home to Switzerland the next night and asked us if we would be willing to keep an eye on Naga and to ask another guest to do the same before we returned home.

Of course we agreed, although we only had another three days left ourselves before we flew home. The following afternoon while we were sunbathing outside our room, she brought Naga over to us along with bowls and tinned dog food and our short period of 'ownership' began.

Naga had a good sniff around our room and then proceeded to lie on the patio outside our door and that night came back, obviously liking the spot. Sadly, that was the last time we ever saw him.

The following morning, Naga was nowhere to be seen. We assumed he had gone walkabout, but when he didn't turn up that evening and nobody else had seen him, we tried to contact the manager to see if he knew what had happened to him.

The hotel manager had gone to Bangkok, but the assistant manager, a Thai man, advised he would ask around. Later, he called back to say that the general manager had requested that Naga be taken away as the hotel was not really suitable for a dog. He explained that staff had taken him to a local temple, so we asked which one as we would like to go and see him and make a donation.

The assistant manager said he would find out, but then explained that rather than taking him to a temple, the staff had, in fact, dropped him off near the bridge that links Phuket to the mainland, where there were several restaurants.

By now we were anxious and our Western mindset came into play. How would Naga survive? He would be lost and confused.

The following day, which was our last full day in Thailand, we arranged to rent a car. We had no idea about what we were going to do if we found him, but that evening we researched online to see what would be involved to get him back to the UK.

It was while doing this research that we first contacted Eve, who advised that there were tens of thousands of dogs on Phuket and not to worry about him. If I did find him, then she knew quite a good temple which did not have too many dogs and might allow him to stay.

After a lot of soul-searching we decided that would be the best solution and we would donate for his upkeep, but first we had to find Naga.

That night Gill wrote in her diary[1]:

> *00:30 and we are off to bed. Thoughts of Naga and thoughts of leaving Thailand running through my head. Oh, for a Lottery win and we could really do wonders, a dog and cat sanctuary here maybe, the suffering we could*

---

1. Gill's diary entries have been reproduced faithfully throughout this book and left unedited

*end, and to educate people about spaying etc. Dreams can come true can't they?*

The following morning, I drove to where we'd been told Naga had been dropped off and went from restaurant to restaurant using very basic pigdin Thai to ask if anybody had seen a white dog. Everywhere the answer was the same: nobody had seen a dog answering Naga's description. I continued to search the area calling out his name but no sign at all.

On returning home we wrote emails and letters to the hotel's head office, but received no replies. In those days there were no laws at all protecting animals, and it would be another sixteen years before that happened.

Six months later we went back to Phuket for a second holiday and, sadly, we learned what really happened to Naga. Gill describes this in Chapter 5. Looking back, it's fair to say that Naga did not die in vain. Although it would be another five years before we were able to move to Thailand, his death and the circumstances surrounding it were what inspired us to try to do something to end all this needless suffering.

It did sour our previous opinion of Thailand and Thai people, but of course we were naïve. Nowhere is perfect and people are the same all over the world. Good and bad.

What happened to Naga brought home to us the real situation for stray animals in Thailand. Most tourists never see beyond the beaches, but there is a whole different world out there.

In reality, Naga suffered the same fate that many other dogs and cats have suffered and probably still do.

In our Soi Dog Foundation education pamphlets for tourists, we warn about befriending stray dogs and cats and particularly about letting them follow you into your hotel grounds or room. An act of apparent kindness could, in effect, be signing that animal's death warrant.

When we made the decision to move to Thailand it was never going to be a normal retirement, but it was Naga's tragic story that drove that and started us on the road to helping strays.

# Introduction

I am just Gill and this is my story. I hope that this book will inspire you to try to make a difference.

In an interview shortly before my death, I said I will not be one of those people who go to the grave saying 'if only'.

I am nothing special. I'm just an ordinary person who tried to do something about the stray dogs and cats of Thailand. Whether I or my legacy will influence change is not the most important thing.

If everybody just tried to make a difference in this world then together we would change it, and my God does it need changing.

If this book inspires just one person to make a difference then it will be worthwhile.

# A Yorkshire lass

If this is going to be a book about me, then before we go looking at how Soi Dog came to be, I think it makes sense, albeit briefly, to look at what brought me first to Thailand and then to devote my life to trying to help that country's stray dogs and cats.

To do that, we have to go back to the very beginning, as I firmly believe that every little event in our lives has an effect on the path we take. Whether it's choices we make or those that are thrust upon us, they can drastically change how our lives work out.

I also believe that although there is no doubt that our physical attributes and even our susceptibility to illnesses and diseases are inherited from one parent or another (as my own physical ailments prove), our personalities are a different matter.

Although some scientists believe that many key personality traits are also inherited, most also agree that our upbringing, particularly in our early years, has a big influence on how we develop.

I also strongly believe that the choices and decisions made, both for us and by us, will determine how our lives turn out. If you think about it, even the seemingly smallest of decisions can be life-changing if you follow them back.

The first major event in my life occurred in the spring of 1958, nine months before my birth. My mother, who was volunteering at a youth club, had an affair with a fellow volunteer while her husband was overseas in the army.

I mention this only because the circumstances and the subsequent decisions made did influence my personality for the rest of my life. Had I been conceived a few years later when abortion became legal in the UK, I imagine it is highly unlikely I would have been born at all, but in the late 1950s, especially for a good Christian family, it was out of the question.

The choice was simple: you either kept the child and accepted the disgrace or were sent away to have the child and give it up for adoption.

According to the official application to give me up for adoption, as that was the choice made in my case, in July 1958 my mother wrote to her husband, who was serving in Malaysia fighting the communists, and to her surprise he applied for leave and was flown home.

The army agreed that he would be permanently stationed in England and the couple decided to settle down and make a go of it. According to the official adoption application, the condition was that he would never have to see me and be reminded of the circumstances of my birth and that I would be adopted. In those days, the natural father had no say at all.

So it was that my mother was packed off in disgrace to the north of England so that nobody, other than the closest family, would be aware of what had happened.

I was born on 29 January 1959 in Otley General Hospital, so am officially a Yorkshire lass.

The first two months of my life were spent with my mother at the mother-and-baby home in Leeds, where the formal application to have me adopted was made.

I have always been told that those first weeks are when the mother-and-baby bond is formed and is the reason why mothers, both human and animal, will often give their lives to save their child.

Although it may come across as self-pity, I'm sure many other adoptees can associate with feelings and questions such as 'Why did my mother not want me then?' and 'What was wrong with me?'

Believe me, it leaves you with a deeply rooted insecurity that is extremely difficult to dislodge. It's certainly had an impact on my life and my relationship with people and animals, which is why I include it here.

My mother went on to have three more children with her husband, apparently becoming a headmistress of a girls' school and a pillar of the community.

In stark contrast to those popular TV shows that show happy people reunited with their natural parents, when many years later John traced my natural mother for me, her reaction was very clear.

I was from another life and no way did she want to meet me or have anybody, particularly her legitimate children, learn of what had happened. This must never come out. She was prepared to write to me only.

As far as I was concerned, this was rejection a second time. The letter was torn up and that was the end of it. Probably because they feared I might try to contact them, they did tell their other now adult children about me and I did meet the eldest son and his wife on one occasion, when they shared photos of my mother with me and told me more about her. The other two siblings, like my mother, did not want to know me.

My birth certificate, which I first saw more than thirty years later after John encouraged me to find out about my past, indicates that I was named

Deborah Hirst (my mother's married name). My father does not appear on the certificate, although he was named on the adoption application.

John also traced that side of my family. My natural father was already dead and had died of lung cancer at the age of fifty-six (another lesson not learned).

When I spoke to my half-brother, Kim, on the phone, he told me he would speak to his aunt – if my story was true, she was one person who would know.

The next day he called me back and told me that his aunt had confirmed it. That was the start of a long-lasting friendship, and I was to visit Kim and my other relatives on several occasions. In fact, Kim actually took the brave step of crossing the Watford Gap and coming north to visit me on my fortieth birthday.

I became godmother to his daughter, not a position I am best qualified to fill, and of course these days more an honour.

On my first visit, Kim met me on the station platform and did not need to hold up the sign he had prepared. He could tell it was me as I looked so much like our father.

My dad's best friend burst into tears when he saw me as he said it was like seeing Ron again. Aunt, as she was called in the family, told me the whole story and also that my dad had really loved my mother and never really came to terms with what had happened, including me being given away.

Anyway, back to my childhood. My adoptive mum and dad met me on 18 March 1959 and I was officially adopted on 20 March and renamed Gillian Margaret Clark.

With so many babies available, checks on new parents were nowhere near as thorough as they are today. Whether my adoptive mother would have got through the exhaustive interviews carried out these days I have no idea. They never made any secret of the fact that I was adopted, which I agree with. Dad certainly loved me and I loved my dad more than anybody else in my life until I met John.

Dad was outgoing and would talk to everybody and anybody on any topic you can imagine, even if, on occasion, to the point of boring them to death.

Mum, on the other hand, was a totally different kettle of fish, and how he put up with her, I'll never know.

As I recall, she was miserable and domineering in the main, with few if any close friends. She never let my father forget that it was his fault she could not have children of her own or failed to tell me how grateful I should be that they had given me a good home.

My father was a strict disciplinarian, but I believe Dad generally acted on the instructions of my mother. John says I show my dad in too good a light, as he could and should have stood up to my mother. However, I don't want to paint too bad a picture as, for the most part, mine was a normal and happy childhood, whatever normal is.

My father's family were all great fun and my grandfather, due to lacking a grandson, decided I could be the surrogate and so instilled in me a love for all sport.

Every Saturday afternoon we would sit in front of the TV and I would be glued to BBC TV's popular sports round-up programme Grandstand, which was televised every Saturday afternoon from noon until 5 p.m. This was a time when the BBC was the main sports channel and footballers got paid in wage packets.

Grandad would sit me on his knee and explain all the rules and regulations of whatever sport was on. Tall and big for my age, I became very much a tomboy and far preferred kicking a football around with the boys than playing silly 'girlie' games.

People often ask me what part animals played in those early days. As a child, I was never allowed to have a dog (my dream) or a cat, but did own a hamster for a couple of years.

I vividly recall one incident when I was very young. My mother had taken me to the funeral of her mother and on the way home, we got off the bus and were walking back to our house when I saw a dead cat in the gutter. I burst into tears, but my mother then slapped me and sent me straight to bed once we got home because I had cried over the cat rather than my grandmother, who I hardly knew. Crying over animals rather than people – some things never change!

My childhood was fairly uneventful until the age of twelve, when my parents announced we were emigrating to Australia – Perth to be exact. It was my father's dream, although my mother did not appear to share his enthusiasm. In 1971 we became 'Ten Pound Poms', as the scheme to encourage UK migrants to move to Australia was called.

Dad had a job all set up in Perth's town planning department, and both myself and my sister, who had been adopted two years after me, were enrolled into new schools.

School in Perth was not a pleasant experience. The male teacher had a real dislike for Poms and on day one made me stand on my chair and tried to get me to admit that I was a leech and say how bad the UK was.

My stubborn streak, something else that hasn't changed, made me refuse, which led to me frequently being beaten with a ruler on the legs and hands and verbally abused. It doesn't matter what you say or do, I will never change my mind or do something I don't want to do.

Australia turned out to be a short-lived adventure. Dad loved it, but Mum hated it. Friendless and with no inclination to change that situation, she missed her family and demanded that we return to Leeds.

This meant we would have to repay the full cost of our fare to Australia and, of course, the cost of the return journey. In the year we had been away, house prices had soared in the UK, which meant hard times on our return.

However, the big plus was that we would return by sea on the Achille Lauro, the Italian cruise ship made famous by being highjacked by Palestinians in 1985.

This voyage was to have a profound impact on me for one incident that has remained with me forever.

The ship had docked in Cape Town, South Africa, and we had ample time to visit this beautiful city. Not only were there signs stating 'whites only' everywhere, but in one doorway a young black girl, who I guessed was aged around six or seven, was sitting begging with, I assume, her baby brother.

My father gave me his last few rand to give to the girl. As an impressionable thirteen-year-old, who had never witnessed anything like this before, it had a profound impact on the way I was to feel about discrimination and persecution for the rest of my life, whether it be humans or animals. I simply cannot stand by and see any creature, human or otherwise, be bullied without stepping in.

This has got me into trouble on more than one occasion, and at times I have had to be dragged away by friends or spouses as I have very much an 'act first, think later' approach.

The rest of my teenage years flew by. I enjoyed playing hockey, netball, football and going to the youth club to dance to the sounds of the seventies (in my opinion still the best era for music ever, although I'm sure everybody thinks the music in their teenage years was the best).

Academically I was distinctly average and left school with five GCE O levels and five CSEs. Mum saw no value in further education and on the first day of leaving school, she said, 'You need to get a job. Don't think we are going to support you.'

The next day I got a job working as an assistant in a ladies' shoe shop and loved it. Clearly I was good at it as well, as within a few weeks the manager was talking of promotion and a full-time job.

However, this was not to last as my mother had other ideas. 'You need a proper job that's secure,' she said. 'Working as a sales assistant is OK for the holidays, but it's not a career.'

I was told to apply for a job at Barclays Bank, a job that would be 'secure for life', or so I was told. Of course, had I not gone to the bank, it is highly unlikely I would have ever met John or set foot in Thailand. As I say, every decision has an impact on where our lives lead. Is it destiny or just chance? I like to think the former.

Although it was not the career I had wanted, I have always been a people person and enjoyed meeting people. In those early days, banks were still very much customer-orientated and I like to think I was good at it and had a natural head for figures.

I became Barclays Bank's youngest ever head cashier. In those days, regular customers were treated as friends; many older customers would come in on some pretext or another, but really they simply wanted a chat.

As anybody who works in a service industry will know, not all customers were pleasant, and although I was able to handle difficult people fairly well, my short fuse sometimes came to the surface, particularly if a member of my team had been upset.

On one infamous occasion after a particularly obnoxious customer had reduced one of the cashiers to tears, I was severely reprimanded by my manager after rushing out of the bank after the customer, grabbing him in the shopping arcade by his tie, and telling him in no uncertain terms what I would do to certain parts of his anatomy if he ever spoke to a member of my staff like that again.

I remember my manager shook his head and said, 'Gillian, you simply cannot do things like that.' He was right, of course, but that's me, and as I've explained, 'act first, think later' is something I've never been able to change.

At home, relations with my mother did not improve and all I wanted was to move out, but as a sixteen-year-old trainee bank clerk, I wasn't earning enough to find somewhere of my own, even if Mum and Dad *had* permitted it.

Although I had many friends who were boys, I didn't have a real boyfriend and thought it unlikely I would find one as I was big girl, overweight and hardly attractive.

However, again chance was to step in, and through a mutual friend I was introduced to Johnathan, who was fit, good company, and earning good money as a bricklayer, which meant escape.

On 3 June 1978, I became Mrs Gillian Barnes, and with a bank staff mortgage, we were able to move into a nice home in a good part of town and settle into married life.

Looking back, I do feel guilty about marrying Johnathan. I was a good wife and he was the perfect recipient for my growing passion for cookery and baking, which was how I've always liked to relax after work.

I had no desire at that time to have a family, whereas I think in reality that is what Johnathan would have liked. Our sex life had ended abruptly. I suffer from psoriasis, inherited apparently from my natural father, and this had got worse since puberty. The worst affected parts were where there was hair, which meant scalp, under the arms, and, of course, the genital area. One night when being amorous, Johnathan pulled back in disgust and said, 'I'm not going near that.'

As you now know, rejection is a major issue in my life, and you don't get a second chance, so that was the end of our sexual relationship, and from that night on, we slept in separate rooms.

Our relationship became more like brother and sister than a husband and wife. We got on well enough and money was not an issue. Other than having a mortgage, I have grown up believing you should never borrow and only buy something when you could afford it, so have never experienced debt.

We had a good social life as well as good holidays and cars. My day-to-day life was dominated by work, followed by cookery in the evenings, and on Saturdays I fulfilled my passion for riding horses . . . fast.

A group of us would meet up most Saturdays at the stables and go off for a ride, stopping off at country pubs on the way back. This resulted in me occasionally falling off as I was very new to alcohol and didn't have my first alcoholic drink until my early twenties, although I have since tried to make up for lost time.

My favourite horse was a retired racehorse named Jack. The feeling of riding across a field at full gallop has to be experienced to be fully appreciated. It is an amazing feeling and one that I would miss when physically I was no longer able to ride.

For love at home, I went elsewhere – cats. I had always wanted a dog (a Doberman, to be precise), but I was sensible enough to realise that as I was out at work all day it would not be fair. But cats? Well, that was different.

My first cat was Crystal, a silver half-Persian with a personality exactly the same as mine; in other words, she was totally screwed up and we became soulmates.

In addition, I then got Elsa, a white Persian, who I allowed to have a litter of kittens, and I kept two of them, Raffles and Pippa. I'm happy to say I did then have them all neutered, but of course with what I know now I would not have bought them in the first place but rather would have gone to the local rescue centre.

These cats became my babies. Crystal rarely left my side and would always know when I was near home and apparently jump up by the door to await my return when I was still a mile or two away.

She was always there for me, and even though she was a problem, spraying on the stairs rather than in her litter tray being just one of her less desirable habits, I forgave her anything and simply covered the stair carpet with plastic sheeting.

The strange thing was that when John and I moved in together some years later, this lifelong habit stopped immediately.

In 1988, I had my first brush with death when I was one of five people in Leeds who contracted a severe form of salmonella. This was the time when

MP Edwina Currie was receiving heavy criticism for warning people about salmonella being in most British eggs. We had all eaten at the same restaurant and, you guessed it, the bacteria was traced to the mayonnaise that we ate which had been made with raw eggs. Two of the people sadly died, and I lost a lot of blood and half my body weight before I recovered.

I had never been a big meat eater but the result of this illness was to leave me with an intolerance for animal fats. Since then, my stomach can detect chicken stock fairly rapidly, for example, in a way I shall leave to your imagination.

Other than this, my twenties and early thirties continued uneventfully. However, in the late 1980s and early 1990s, the banking industry was changing rapidly and the 'job for life' was no more. Bank branches were closing and the focus turned more to selling other financial products. I was transferred to head office in Leeds to manage one of the new customer service teams, which, compared with the old days, was something of a misnomer. I had a good team, though, and we made the best of a bad job.

However, something was going on with my body and I was frequently in a lot of pain with my neck, shoulders, and arm down to my wrist. I was given various courses of drugs and diagnoses ranged from arthritis (at my age?) to something I'd never heard of, and which was not even at that time officially recognised by the medical profession: repetitive strain injury.

One specialist advised that he believed the years of counting money and lifting heavy bags of change had caused irreversible damage to the joints in my arms. I had surgery on my wrist, as my right hand had become quite useless, and various treatments on my arms leading to extended periods off work.

Unable to ride – and, let's face it, there is only so much cooking you can do for one person as I did not eat sweet things and preferred salad – I took up walking, with afternoon visits to the pub when I was bored and needed company.

I would often sit and chat with a guy called Alan who was also off work for an extended period, and we became good friends.

I continued to call in at this pub on occasions on my way home even when back working and would meet up with Alan for an after-work beer and a natter, and so it was that one day in 1992 an event occurred that would change my life and the life of an awful lot of dogs and cats forever.

# Meeting John

I walked into our local as usual that evening. The Dexter Pub was only a stone's throw away from our house. In those days, if you walked in the side entrance, immediately on entering the pub there was a ledge on the wall to the right of the door where two or three people could sit on bar stools and put their drinks on the ledge. This was Alan's spot. There he was as usual, only this time he was talking to a tall, thin man who looked pleasant enough. This man was sitting opposite Alan with legs crossed and holding a cigarette in a somewhat limp-wristed way. My initial impression was that he was probably gay and had an appalling dress sense, as he was wearing a very old-fashioned nylon combination shirt and jumper. He gave me a lovely smile, though, which I returned, and certainly he seemed pleasant enough. I always get on really well with gay men, but on this occasion my usually unerring first impression was to prove incorrect as it was soon clear he was not gay. He did, however, have no sense of fashion and was nice so I got two thirds right.

Alan introduced us. John, as he was called, apparently worked for the same company as Alan, and Alan had suggested he call in for a drink as John had recently separated from his wife and had bought a small cottage in the village down the road from the pub, where he was now living with his dog, Max. A dog! OK, a Cavalier King Charles spaniel is no Doberman, but a dog is a dog and all dogs need walks.

The company John worked for ran twenty-four hours a day, 365 days a year, and although he got a generous amount of days off, when he was working, he was away more than twelve hours a day.

Poor Max would be shut up all day, and so I suggested that if John and Max were happy with it, I could take Max for a walk when I was not working, which was happening ever more frequently.

There was nothing wrong with my legs, and taking Max on long walks not only gave me pleasure, but Max clearly loved it as well. Many people think of Cavaliers as lap dogs, but they retain a lot of their ancestors' gundog instincts, and certainly Max could keep going all day.

As I have mentioned, although John worked long shifts, he also had a lot of days off, with six teams covering the complicated shift pattern. Over the course of a year, he had two days off for every day worked, including a block of seventeen days off every six weeks. Not bad if you can get it.

John suggested that maybe we could go on walks together when he wasn't working, and it wasn't long before we started going further afield to my beloved Yorkshire Dales.

What had started as two-hour local walks to the park and back became full-day outings. These walks inevitably meant that we came home through Otley and we would stop at the Junkie, as the Junction Inn was known: a dog-friendly pub that just happened to serve the best ever pint of Timothy Taylor's Landlord, probably the finest beer known to man.

There is no doubt that our friendship was deepening, and during that summer John would also come around to the house at weekends and join us for barbeques. When John was working, I would leave him meals to come home to and even, at his request, took him on food-shopping lessons on one occasion.

There was never any hint of how John really felt. He was always the perfect gentleman, even though he was to tell me after we got together that it had been love at first sight for him.

Our conversations got deeper and I found myself being able to speak about anything and everything with him. I also learned that he was very similar to me in many respects.

He had had a loveless childhood. His mother and father had met at the end of the war in Holland. She had been married to a Dutchman, who had been shot in front of her at their house. He had only learned of this quite recently and believes his mother never really got over it. John thinks that his father was an escape for her, a way to escape the memories and start an entirely new life in another country.

When John was still a baby, his mother became seriously ill and had a kidney removed. John and his elder sister, Karin, were taken care of by relatives, and he never remembers a close bond with his mother as a child, no physical affection at all.

His father was very domineering and abusive. Trips to the garage to be beaten with the washing stick were common. People handle things differently. I became extremely outgoing and hid my insecurities by, in effect, pretending to be the opposite. If I was upset, I showed it. John, on the other hand, became withdrawn and built walls. He had learned not to show emotion and to hide his true feelings. Extremely unhealthy and something I was determined to try to change, whereas John was equally determined to try to change my explosions of anger and emotion when things upset me. They always say that when you enter into a relationship, accept people as they are and don't try to change them. They will change themselves if things are right.

Now I am no psychologist, but I am sure they would have had a field day with us. They say abused children often become abusers themselves. With John, it was the opposite. Even as a child, when like me he was big for his age, he became almost a protector of other kids who were bullied. Just like me, he grew up hating abuse and cruelty, and there is no doubt in my mind that he was meant to work with abused animals. He would also often get into trouble for having stones or sweet-wrappers and other rubbish in his pockets. He had, what I assume, is some form of obsessive compulsive behaviour in that he hated seeing even inanimate objects on their own, so would bring them home, which, of course, got him into trouble with his parents, who would demand where he got the money from to buy the sweets as obviously nobody would pick up empty wrappers. His antisocial behaviour developed further and his schoolwork was suffering. A psychiatrist was brought in, who advised he was extremely intelligent and his IQ was well into Mensa territory, which I'm sure was fascinating to his parents but not what they were looking for. The decision was taken to pack him off to boarding school, not an experience he remembers with any fondness. He did, however, start to excel at school, and his housemaster advised his parents that he should easily gain entrance to Oxford or Cambridge.

But John had other ideas and got himself expelled for something he didn't actually do. A fire had started at a disused mill near the school that boys used for secret smoking. John was often guilty of smoking there but had not been responsible for the fire. In the public-school system, you did not grass on somebody else, so even though he knew who was responsible he took the rap and went home.

He was allowed to return to take his exams, but with life intolerable, at the age of fifteen he walked out of the front door with a half-crown coin (12.5 new pence in post-decimalisation currency) and set off to London.

Walking the first stage to Doncaster, he knocked on a door on the road leading to the A1 to ask for a glass of water, and the lovely couple, who had a son at university, invited him in, gave him a slap-up meal, and then the dad drove him to the service station at the A1 junction and told him to approach lorry drivers at the café rather than thumb a lift. It was a good tip and it wasn't long before he got a ride. They drove through the night, arriving in the capital in the early hours of the morning.

It was summer and, determined to find work, the first thing he did was to go into a phone box to find the address of the youth employment office. There on the shelf somebody had left a wallet with around £30 in it. A lot of money in those days. Of course he should have handed it in, and did in fact post the wallet and the rest of the contents to the person whose name and address were inside, but with no money in his pocket it seemed almost like it was meant to be.

His guardian angel was certainly working overtime. In those days, sleeping rough in London was not tolerated by the authorities, who were quick to move you on, and there were plenty of vultures on the prowl looking for young victims.

John was approached numerous times on his first nights alone in the capital. A retired schoolmaster approached him and John gave him the usual brush-off, but the man persisted and told him he was trying to help him, something he did regularly, and keep him out of trouble until he got on his feet. He gave John a room to stay in, and within a few days he found himself a job earning the princely sum of £6 a week. He sent a postcard to his parents telling them he was safe, and for the next three years split his time between jobs in London and Leeds, focusing on becoming a hotel manager. It was while working and living at a hotel in Leeds as a trainee manager that he was to meet Ann, who was his first relationship, and shortly after his nineteenth birthday, only a few months after meeting, they married at Leeds Registrar office with just a taxi driver and a work colleague as witnesses. Nine months later and John's eldest son was born. Working as a trainee manager and having to live in was not conducive to supporting a family, and John went to working on the buses and later at a chemical plant in Castleford, working every available hour to buy a house and car and provide the young family with a decent lifestyle.

Looking back, John would be the first to admit that he had become a lost soul searching for love and a purpose in life. That he should not have married and become a father at such a young age he accepts, but then his sons would not have been born and the very twisted and tortuous path his life was taking would not eventually have led him to me and our life together.

His search certainly took him down some strange paths. A few years into the marriage, John and his wife joined the Mormon Church. This was again a part of looking for a purpose to life, and as with anything he did, John never did anything by halves. It was all or nothing for him in everything he did. As a result, within three years he found himself made bishop of the church, but the only problem was that although he could appreciate the way the church looked to strengthen the family unit and the close friendships that developed between members, inside he knew he did not believe in any of the tenets on which the church had been founded and realised how hypocritical he was being. So he left the church, and before long also his wife, as their marriage, which had been hanging by a thread, was now reaching its end, with the church becoming a division.

In the meantime, John had got his first dog and then a second, both Cavalier King Charles spaniels, and was taking an interest in dogs generally, including the show circuit. It was here that he met Sheila, and it was not long after he and Ann split up that Sheila and he set up home together.

It was an unlikely relationship, and although it lasted a few years, both of them had been in unhappy marriages and it was their common interest in dogs that brought them together. Having a common interest can certainly help a relationship, but without love it is not likely to last, and when the common interest also goes then the relationship is definitely doomed. Sheila lost interest in breeding and showing dogs and also wanted John to get his dogs rehomed. They split up and John bought a small cottage in Shadwell and met me at the Dexter Pub one summer evening in 1992 – little did we know what adventures lay ahead.

## Together at last

There is no doubt that my feelings for John were growing, and it was one evening in York only a few months after we had first met that things abruptly changed.

We had decided to take a friend of ours who had recently been widowed for an afternoon out in her favourite city, York.

John, myself, Johnathan, and Ruby met up at Cross Gates Station and took the train for the short trip to somewhere that would become one of our favourite places. Here we did the usual touristy things, calling into souvenir shops in the afternoon before arriving at a pub called the Punch Bowl in Stonegate.

There, in the back room laughing and joking together, I found my eyes constantly drawn to John's. It is hard to describe, but all of a sudden I knew I loved him and I could tell he loved me. Trying to behave normally with Johnathan and Ruby, who of course were blissfully unaware of what was going on unspoken between me and John, was not easy, to put it mildly.

We decided to go for an Indian meal, and as we walked along Stonegate, Ruby and Johnathan were a few yards ahead of me and John. Our hands touched, and although this may sound like a line from a *Mills and Boon* novel, it was like a jolt of electricity passing through me.

I whispered to John, 'Please stop,' but stop what? He hadn't done anything or said anything up to that point, but we both just knew.

He whispered back, 'I'm sorry, but I'm in love with you and I think you feel the same way.' Of course, he was right, but with my husband a few yards in front of me, now was not the time for us to profess our love for each other.

The rest of the walk passed in silence. I don't know how I managed to eat my food or put on a show that all was normal. Inside, I just wanted to be alone with John.

After dinner, we walked back to the station, and because Ruby had had a little too much to drink, it was decided that John would take her home.

I decided I would drop Johnathan off and then go check on her. With Ruby parked on a chair in her living room, John and I went to the kitchen to make us all coffee.

You can guess the rest; as soon as we were in the kitchen, we fell into each other's arms and kissed passionately.

That was as far as it went, but not before Ruby, who had decided we probably needed help finding the coffee, walked in, and to say she was shocked is an understatement.

I persuaded her that it was nothing serious and not to say anything to Johnathan, but made arrangements to see John at his house the next day to talk things through.

The next day, I drove to his house in a mixed state of emotions: excitement, trepidation, nervousness. Would he say it had all been a big mistake and tell me we should stop seeing each other?

I needn't have worried; we were immediately in each other's arms and inevitably soon in his bed. In the biblical sense, I had only ever 'known' two men. Johnathan, of course, but that had ended years before, and a brief fling with a married policeman who I had coincidentally met walking in the Dales, but that was over almost as soon as it began.

This was the first time I had experienced what I would term as real lovemaking, with somebody who was more intent on my needs than his own. I had never experienced anything like it, and I like to think neither had John.

My insecurities were never far away, though. Was this just a fling? John had already been married twice. His shifts meant he never worked more than three days or nights consecutively and always had at least two weekdays off every week.

I was now, on the insistence of my employers at the bank, on long-term leave as it became increasingly obvious that my disabilities were work-related.

The result was that our walking days increased. Meeting up one day a week became a day spent indoors, and we maintained this practice until we moved to Thailand.

Our days at home together consisted of drawing the curtains, locking the doors, and shutting the rest of the world out. These days were spent lovemaking, curling up and watching movies, and taking it in turns to prepare a special dinner.

John was a good cook, even if he followed recipes exactly rather than relying on taste. I guess this was the industrial chemist in him, where the concoctions had to follow precise recipes. He was certainly ambitious, though, and made some delicious meals.

We still went walking every week as well and covered most of the Yorkshire Dales, North Yorkshire moors, and the Lake District. We were joined by a new puppy called Junkie, named after our – and later his – favourite pub. It didn't matter where we parked in Otley, Junkie would always pull us directly there.

The idea behind getting a puppy was to give Max a friend, although initially he didn't take kindly to having an annoying puppy spoiling his routine. Max quickly found that although Junkie would follow him upstairs by the wooden open staircase, he was initially too frightened to come down again, so when Max had had enough, he would lead Junkie upstairs, turn around, and come back down again to enjoy some peace – if not quiet, as Junkie would then sit at the top step and cry to come down.

Over the next few years, though, until Max passed away, they became inseparable, and Max rekindled his own puppy playfulness again.

Although in Thailand we have gone too far the other way, I would always recommend every home has two dogs.

This way of life and our secret affair was to continue for nearly two years. John wanted me to tell Johnathan and for us to move in together permanently. Although I felt the same way, my insecurities were always there and have never fully gone away, which is John's fault.

Men just don't get the emotional needs that women need, particularly this woman. How could I be sure he would not get fed up of me, just as he had before with his previous wives? I was in a loveless marriage; my future career was totally in the hands of the bank, their lawyers, and doctors.

I owned my own house, having paid off the staff mortgage in only a few years. John was still paying maintenance to his first wife and had forfeited all claims to the houses he had shared with her and his second wife on the basis that their marriage was a clean split.

It may sound mercenary, but being secure was incredibly important to me, and my insecurities were telling me I could rapidly lose everything.

The reality, though, was that nearly two years later, John had never indicated he wanted to end the relationship, just the opposite, and although our days in and out were magical, saying goodbye at the end of them was becoming increasingly harder.

I did not want to go home. John had stopped pestering me to leave Johnathan, so it must have come as something of a shock when as we again said goodbye one day, I told him I was going to tell my husband that our marriage was over.

I can't say that I wasn't frightened at the prospect. Even though Johnathan had never been violent towards me, he was a powerful man and had a short fuse. We had lived separate lives for years, more as brother and sister, but I was still his wife and I knew he was not going to take the news well.

In fact, that was an understatement. He went crazy and became threatening. Eventually he calmed down and I had to agree to stop seeing John until I left permanently.

Lawyers were consulted and I agreed that my husband could have the house, even though I had paid for it, and that I would make no claims on him at all in return for him agreeing to a divorce.

I kept my Barclays shares, which I had been building up over the years, and I also had a secret savings account which Johnathan knew nothing about. It was my little bit of independence and security for a rainy day.

I did, of course, secretly continue to see John, including searching for another house because I wanted to be well away from Johnathan.

In July 1994, two years after we first met, John and I moved into our first home together. We bought a house on the Leeds to Wetherby Road in a village halfway between the two. Although the house was on the main road, it overlooked fields behind and only had one neighbour. It was also situated next to the Leeds Country Way so we could literally walk about ten yards and we were in the countryside.

John moved in first and the following day I hired a man with a van to move my personal possessions. My three cats came in the car with me. Raffles, the only boy, had sadly died the previous year from heart failure.

It was going to be interesting. All three were house cats and had never seen a dog before, while Max and Junkie were completely unfamiliar with cats.

As it turned out, Junkie wanted to play with them, but the cats soon put him in his place and there were no real dramas at all.

The strange thing was that Crystal stopped spraying, and I can only think she sensed the change in atmosphere. Johnathan had never been cruel to her as far as I knew but equally he was not a 'cat person'. Maybe Crystal now just felt happy because I was happy, and happy I was.

I was also now a full-time housewife. Initially, it had been agreed that I would be given early retirement because of ill health, but the bank's head office was not in agreement and my situation was turning into a landmark case.

Nobody, including my own specialist who had first diagnosed it, wanted to agree that the cause of my incapacity was down to this still-new condition known as a repetitive strain injury as this would set a precedent.

In addition, the bank's pension scheme doctors said that while they accepted that I could not work *now*, it was not possible to confirm that the condition was permanent. The net result was that I was offered voluntary redundancy on better terms than normal and registered as disabled by the government.

The pain in my shoulders was constant, and the colder the weather, the worse it got. An arm brace and sling were fairly constant items of apparel, but at least the rest of me was fine.

Although John and I were together, some things did not change, and our weekly day in was sacred. Regular walks in the Dales and beyond also continued whatever the weather. I remember one walk when there was thick snow on the Fells. As we headed down back to the car, the snow began to fall heavily and it was heads-down into a blizzard. Suddenly, John noticed that Max was not behind him and had to go back up the hill searching for him. Fortunately, he was not that far behind, but he was unable to move. Cavaliers, like all spaniels, have feathered legs, and the snow had gradually built up until both front legs had giant snowballs attached to them – poor Max was unable to move. For some reason, Junkie was unaffected, but John had to carry the exhausted Max back to the car, where we managed to thaw out the, by now solid, ice balls. After that we were always careful to ensure the same thing did not happen again by regularly removing bits of ice and snow that were drawn to his feathers.

We would also have occasional weekends away in London. John had introduced me to musical theatre and I loved it from the start. The first show he took me to was the original production of Cats.

Every six weeks John had a break of seventeen days from work and would regularly book a long weekend where we would take in a matinee and an evening performance on the Thursday and Saturday and another evening performance on the Friday. Five shows in three days in effect. Over the top? Maybe, but as I said, John never did things by halves.

We always stayed at the Regent Palace Hotel, which has since closed, where you could stay very cheaply right in the heart of London's West End, literally yards from Piccadilly Circus and walking distance to the theatres. Since closing, parts of the hotel were sold off and it lost that character, but it will always hold a special place in my memory.

Over the next few years we saw every musical there was to see and our favourites many times over. *Miss Saigon* became my personal favourite, and no matter how many times I saw it, I was always a wreck at the end of it. John commented more than once that I should not bother with eye makeup when going to see it. It was probably the connection of a mother giving away her child that got to me. How many times did I see it? No idea; we lost count and John even contacted Cameron Mackintosh, the producer, and got tickets to go see Lea Salonga, the famous Filipina singer and actress, in New York, after Cameron had told me at Leeds Playhouse that she was returning to close the show there in 2001.

It was my forty-second birthday and my penultimate one in the UK. John had told me we were going away somewhere to celebrate, but not where. I was guessing London when we got a taxi down to Leeds Station. But no, we were boarding a train bound for Manchester. Manchester Airport I guessed, but where, then?

Halfway through the journey, John, who had said he was going to the loo, came back and his face was grey. I asked him what the matter was as he looked about to have a heart attack, and he told me he had not got my passport. Had he dropped it at Leeds Station or in the taxi?

Poor John was panic-stricken. I phoned his mother, who was staying at our house pet-sitting, in case he had left it there. He told me he had been hiding it so I didn't guess we were going overseas. I don't know what possessed John's mum to look there, but she decided to check his dressing gown pocket and there it was. We were now well on the way to Manchester Airport and the passport was in Leeds.

I called my sister, who lived several miles away, and she and her husband volunteered to pick my passport up and drive to the airport, although it was unlikely they would arrive in time before our scheduled departure.

When we arrived at the airport, John went to the British Airways desk and explained the position. They were very helpful and said if the passport did not arrive on time they would fly us to London and we could get another flight from there, noting I still had no idea where we were going.

Literally five minutes before departure time, my sister drew up at the door and dashed in with the passport. The British Airways staff ran us to the gate and it was only then that I saw New York at the gate entrance. The BA stewardess did not realise that I didn't know where I was going and she promptly burst into tears.

We had a great weekend away and the whole thing really summed up John. Capable of making dreams come true, but incredibly forgetful and careless at the same time.

My only concern once the excitement had died down was that I had already booked a surprise trip to New York several months later for John's birthday! Fortunately, we both loved New York, and the trip I had booked for him was very different.

The habit of leaving notes for one another also continued. When John was on nights, I prepared a meal for him and would always leave a note for him to read. He would always leave one for me on my pillow.

Sometimes, I would leave him one in his coffee cup and always find one in mine when I got up. If all this sounds like a perfect relationship then in most respects it was. There was nothing we would not do for each other. However, my insecurities were always there, and I needed to know constantly that he loved me and would not be leaving me. I needed affection and to feel loved.

John, of course, was the opposite. Brought up in a family where outward affection was not shown or expressed, it was foreign to his nature to be outwardly affectionate and that never changed. Showing or displaying affection is not something John appeared able to do, but it was what I needed the most.

He would argue that actions spoke louder than words, but I needed to hear it and feel it. When I didn't, I would feel unloved, and that led to me brooding and eventually exploding.

After making up, John would always promise to try harder but put it down to a typical *Men Are from Mars, Women Are from Venus* situation. That didn't help me. Why do men, particularly John, have to analyse everything and try to come up with rational explanations? I had to express how I felt, and if something was upsetting me it had to be said – and often angrily.

John hates confrontation but when he does lose it, he really does lose it, and I was good at making him angry.

Over the years, we were to have frequent, often violent, rows which were a blight on our relationship, but that doesn't stop me considering myself the luckiest person alive to have met him, and deep down I knew he loved me.

I just wished he would show it more.

I had already told John frequently that he knew what sort of person he had married and you can't change people. Of course, he would say I should also have accepted this about him, but that's different …

There were other areas where he did change me, though. I had always hated Christmas. John was Father Christmas personified. Even before we got together, he would designate our day nearest Christmas as our Christmas Day. After our first such Christmas Day, it became my favourite time of the year as well.

John had traditions that had to be followed, from hanging up stockings and the number of presents Santa would leave in them (eight) to not being allowed to open other presents, which were arranged around the tree before going to bed.

I would wake up like an excited child asking *has he been?* Of course he had, so John would go downstairs and make a cup of tea and let the dogs and cats (if they wanted) up into the bedroom.

The dogs also got their own stockings. We took turns at opening presents, which were non-expensive items. Then it was dressed and downstairs. While I checked over the food and turned on the oven in preparation, John would pour us a glass of Bucks Fizz and we would then go into the lounge where the Christmas tree was surrounded with presents.

Not only would we give presents for each other, but also the dogs, cats, fish, Santa Claus, you name it. Other traditions included watching the same films every year on TV on Christmas Eve, notably the original *Scrooge* with Alastair Sim and *It's A Wonderful Life*, neither of which I had seen before meeting John.

Prior to that we would head to York and spend an hour just wandering the streets, which had a real Dickensian Christmas feel to them, none more so than our beloved Stonegate with views of York Minster at one end with bells ringing and of course the Punch Bowl at the other, where we would have a couple of drinks in front of a blazing fire before heading home again.

In the days leading up to Christmas, John would read me a chapter of Charles Dickens' *A Christmas Carol* every night, complete with character voices.

From being somebody who had little time for Christmas, he converted me into someone that wholeheartedly threw themselves into it.

I loved it, and even in tropical Thailand, Christmas Eve and Christmas Day were two days of the year when the doors were shut, the aircon turned up full, and any foreigner we knew who was spending Christmas on their own invited around to celebrate it with us.

The only thing John and I disagreed on was Brussels sprouts. John's had to be firm and just cooked. For some reason, I liked my sprouts boiled to within an inch of their lives. So I always had a separate pan of sprouts just for me.

The only thing that changed in Thailand was having the dogs upstairs, as getting up to ten or more dogs and half a dozen cats on the bed at once would have been somewhat chaotic, to put it mildly, although until he died Junkie did, of course, still come up and have his own stocking.

I had never wanted children – I hate kids! I had certainly never wanted them with Johnathan.

John had had three sons already and was enjoying his life for the first time, and anyway, he'd already had a vasectomy. That did not stop me thinking if only we had met earlier how different things might have been, but we hadn't, and my animals are my babies and probably why I take their loss harder than most people.

Over the next four years, firstly Elsa, then Pippa, and finally my beloved Crystal, who I was sure would not die before me, all passed, along with dear Max.

Crystal's death affected me quite badly and it took a long time to come to terms with. I know they say you should feel the same about all your pets and, indeed, children, but I am sure I am not alone in saying that you bond more with some than others. So it was with Crystal. I treated all my cats the same, but there will never be another Crystal; she was as difficult and grouchy as I was, which is probably why we were so close.

Now I'm sure you are finding all this fascinating but are also asking yourself what does all this have to do with Soi Dog Foundation and Thailand? Bear with me; we will get there next . . .

# Marriage and Thailand

Johnathan and I were officially divorced in September 1994 and John's divorce was finalised the following January. At that point neither of us felt any immediate need to get married, although I did want John to show his commitment to me and John wanted me to have security in case something happened to him.

Again, typical *Men Are from Mars, Women Are from Venus* scenario, even if the net result was the same. We had previously married in registry offices and although I have nothing against them, we both wanted something different this time. So we decided to get married overseas. But where?

I was far more widely travelled than John, and as much as I loved the Caribbean, weddings there seemed to be conducted almost in a conveyor-belt fashion.

Getting married in a chapel in Las Vegas was my idea of hell. John had always had a desire to visit Asia. He had had a fascination with Asia going back to school days when he had seen the 1960 film *The World of Susie Wong* at his school's movie night, which was filmed and set in Hong Kong.

It had been the scenes of the city that enthralled him rather than the subject matter.

He had also watched *The King and I*, set in Thailand of course, and had been actively involved in anti-Vietnam war demonstrations when he was working in London and had also studied the history and culture of the country and the reasons for the war.

I had been to India but never to Southeast Asia, so we began to look and see if it was possible to get married out there. We picked up a specialist holiday brochure that featured weddings overseas and found that Thailand was a possibility.

I was a saver, and as I mentioned earlier had a secret account which was for my security and also for being able to surprise John. I loved to surprise him and this continued throughout our life together. So I told him I'd been saving up, and not only were we going to have a special wedding, but also the holiday of a lifetime – and he would finally see Asia.

On later holidays I started keeping a diary, but on this occasion I just kept a scrapbook to remind me of one of the happiest times of my life.

On 19 February 1996, we left a cold and very wintry Leeds for the start of our adventure.

We spent the first night in London, where of course we took in yet another performance of Miss Saigon, before flying out the following afternoon on a British Airways flight to Hong Kong.

It was the first of eight flights and six destinations over the period of a month, all the others being in Thailand.

We didn't realise that the biggest national holiday of the year in Hong Kong, Chinese New Year, had occurred on 19 February and that the island was in what can best be described as 'hangover mode'. Also, although we'd checked average temperatures in Hong Kong in February before we left, the place was undergoing its coldest February in living memory and more than a hundred people had already died of hypothermia.

In reality, it was nowhere near as cold as the UK, but cold enough that we were destined to wear our warm travel clothes for the three-night stay at the Shangri La Kowloon. Had we been two days earlier, our room would have given us a grandstand view of the fireworks display over the harbour.

Hong Kong had come a long way since the 1950s, and other than the ferries and junks bore little resemblance to the Hong Kong street scenes John remembered from his film days.

In addition, he found the smells of the street food nauseating and it looked and tasted nothing like the 'Chinese' food back in Leeds. Fortunately, he was able to find refuge in the hotel restaurant. Street food and markets were my 'thing', and I delighted in trying new tastes and flavours.

If Hong Kong was something of a disappointment, then our next stop, Chiang Mai, was the total opposite.

From the minute we stepped off the plane into that warmth and smiles of the welcoming Thai Airways ground crew, Thailand felt great. With no expectations, we enjoyed every minute of our stay in the city.

Even the tout trying to entice you to go and visit his brother, who would sell you jewellery you could then resell at a huge profit in the UK, was pleasant as he acted as an impromptu guide at a temple we were looking at.

John has never been a great lover of Thai food, but even he found no difficulty in finding meals he could enjoy. I was in seventh heaven. I love chillies and, as John says, I must have an asbestos mouth as I can eat the hottest of foods and enjoy them. I loved Thai food and I loved shopping, so Chiang Mai was like heaven on earth to me.

The one thing we did which, now we know better, should not have done was to visit an elephant centre where you could go on a short trek and then watch these magnificent animals perform tricks and play football for the hordes of tourists cheering them on.

Like many tourists at that time and even today, we were ignorant of the cruelty involved in this business. Now, of course, we know better, but in those days we thought it was just a way to keep former logging elephants in work. Three nights in Chiang Mai seemed too short, but off we went again for the short flight to Mae Hong Sorn, a remote, mountainous province in northern Thailand, where we were booked to spend two nights.

In those days it would have taken many hours by road to reach this then sleepy backwater town near the Myanmar border.

We had booked a full-day excursion to visit the long-necked tribe at a refugee camp reached by long-tail boat, another elephant trek, and visits to more hill tribes and local beauty spots. This elephant trek was to be our last for more reasons than one.

On our next visit to Chiang Mai we visited the Elephant Nature Park, a sanctuary for abused elephants, many of whom had spent their lives doing what we were doing now. There we learned of the abuse and cruelty these beautiful animals go through to serve tourists.

On this trip, however, we had no idea, and this trek started off magically.

John and I were on one elephant and another couple were on the one behind. Later they told us it was very obvious that our elephant had a badly upset stomach. We started off crossing the river and then wandered through quiet jungle paths with our *mahout* singing what I assume were local folk songs.

It was just perfect until our elephant suddenly decided it had had enough and charged off through the jungle and up the hill with the *mahout* vainly chasing after it and shouting for it to stop.

As our elephant ran, the seat contraption we were sitting in began to slide off his back, and I had visions of us falling under the charging elephant and being trampled to death.

John held on to me and told me not to panic. Not to panic! Fortunately, for whatever reason, our elephant stopped and the *mahout* caught up and led us back down to safety.

What we witnessed then gave us our first insight into the real world of elephant trekking. The *mahout* had a metal hammer-like implement with a spike at one end and a flat hammer at the other. He began to beat the elephant with it. I screamed at him to stop and told him that clearly the elephant was not well, although the *mahout* couldn't understand English.

Our guide, who had been waiting for us, said something to him in Thai and then explained to us that the elephant had very thick skin and could not feel the hammer, something which neither John or I believed for one second.

It was our first lesson in learning that under the beautiful façade tourists see, not everything is what it seems in Thailand, particularly when it comes to animals. Whether you are a stray dog or wildlife, Thailand is not somewhere you would want to live.

The sad thing is, of course, that with wildlife there is far more profit to be made by preserving it in its natural habitat and developing eco-tourism than there is in exploiting it.

Other than our brush with death on the back of the elephant, we enjoyed Mae Hong Sorn. What it is like twenty years on I have no idea, but I was certainly glad we saw it when we did.

A quick flight back to Chiang Mai and our fifth flight and fourth destination: Bangkok, the Thai capital. We were staying at the Dusit Thani at the top of Silom Road, but first we had to get there.

Everything that had been said about Bangkok traffic was true, only more so. We had landed in the middle of some international conference and had to endure waiting three hours in a taxi while the likes of our prime minister, John Major, were whisked through the streets.

This was before the Sky Train existed and Bangkok traffic was at its very worst.

On one occasion, we abandoned a taxi and walked back to our hotel. The main purpose of visiting Bangkok was to go to the British Embassy to get official clearance to marry.

The travel company was brilliant. We were parked in an air-conditioned café opposite the embassy while a member of their staff joined the queue. As soon as she was at the front, we were whisked in to swear that we were eligible to marry and get a letter to this effect. In and out in five minutes.

From there, we went to a translation office where the letter was translated, and finally to the Thai Foreign Ministry to have our letter stamped. We were now in a position to get married and the date was set for 13 March at the Dusit Laguna Hotel in Phuket.

We also wanted to see the notorious Patpong area in Bangkok, which was fortunately only a few minutes' walk from the hotel. Why did we want to see the famous street noted for its girlie bars and live sex shows? Quite simply, and without giving the story away, much of the second act of *Miss Saigon* is set there and we wanted to see if it was anything like it was portrayed in the show.

Clearly the writers and set designers had been here as some of the signs were identical and the pimps with their menu cards were everywhere.

But Patpong is no longer the Bangkok capital of sleaze, and its main attraction is now a street market that runs the entire length of the road with the bars little more than a sideshow.

However, it was amusing to see the touts shoving menus with items listed such as 'girl and ping pong balls' or 'girl smoke cigarette' etc. in the faces of middle-aged tourists who were intent only on knocking down the price of the fake Rolex watch on the stall outside. The Engineer (a character in *Miss Saigon*) would be turning in his grave.

As usual, I had found a favourite restaurant, this time a couple of streets from Patpong, and we became good friends with the staff there. It is a practice that has changed little over the years on holiday. We find somewhere we like and tend to stick with it. Very unadventurous, I know.

With the official business out of the way, we did the usual tourist things, avoiding the roads as much as possible. A boat trip on the Chao Phraya River, detouring down canals that gave an impression of life that has changed little over the years.

We visited the Temple of Dawn and the Reclining Buddha, where we had our fortunes told.

The fortune-tellers want not only the day and year of your birth, but also the time, and fortunately this was one question my natural mother *did* answer when I wrote to her. I had started to take a great interest in spiritual matters and knew the importance of such information.

The fortune-teller told me that the next years of my life would be good, but at age forty-five to forty-six, I would have problems, but all would be well again when I was forty-seven.

John, of course, has no faith in any of this, but I do, and this prophecy was to prove to be totally correct.

We departed Bangkok on 5 March for the short flight to Phuket. Little did we know the part this place was to play in our lives in years to come.

We were staying at the Dusit Laguna, where we were also to be married eight days later. Our suitcase, which contained my wedding dress and accessories, had, of course, followed us around, but could now at last be unpacked. Every flight I had been a bag of nerves that the case would be lost or damaged; now at last I could relax and unpack it. Everything was fine.

The hotel was lovely, and we had a great room which was to be requested on every subsequent trip. Room 102 was on the ground floor, the next-to-last room on the right hand side as you looked towards the sea. From its private veranda was a lawn that led to the beach. This suited me fine. I have never been a great lover of sandy beaches so being able to laze on a sunbed on grass overlooking the sea was perfect. The cold UK and Hong Kong were now distant memories.

The hotel staff and our holiday rep were great. Everything had been organised to the last detail for our wedding, and we were able to just relax and do some sightseeing.

I am sure I am not alone in saying that as places develop, you tend to forget what they used to be like. Back in 1996, Phuket was already a major holiday destination, but was nothing like it is today in terms of traffic and roads. What is now known as the 'old airport road' was *the* airport road.

I can't remember if the busy bypass road had yet been started, but I do remember it was a small single carriageway road, and even the original big supermarkets such as Tesco and Big C had not yet been built.

If you wanted foreign food you needed to go to the old town in Phuket Town to a small shop called Sin and Lee. To get to Patong down the coast, you had to drive through what are now back roads in Kamala.

It seems strange to think that only a few years previously, Patong had been a sleepy place, known only to backpackers and reached only by motorcycles over dirt tracks.

It's a shame it did not remain that way. It is the way of the world that backpackers find the best spots and then mass tourism or exclusive luxury resorts follow.

Laguna, where we were staying, had been reclaimed from wasteland left behind by the tin-mining industry. You have to hand it to the Singaporean developer who bought what was considered useless land for a song and transformed it into the resort it was when we first visited.

Five luxury hotels, a golf course, and a small boutique shopping area spread over a wide area of beautiful grounds, with wildlife abounding and linked by lagoons along which little boats would take you from one hotel to another if you so wished.

Today, the hotels still exist, but every bit of land that can be built on has been, with apartment blocks, villas, and townhouses springing up everywhere. The wildlife has largely disappeared and it is hard to see how the infrastructure can support this growth. The truth, of course, is that it can't, but more on that later.

Beyond the resort lay a typical Thai village called Cherngtalay. It had small local shops and a twice-weekly market. One or two enterprising locals had opened up restaurants to try to entice tourists from the Laguna hotels, but it was largely untouched.

Today, the whole area has changed, with more restaurants, shops, and bars catering to the expat and tourist industry than one can count, but at least it has not gone the way of Patong … yet.

In those early days, the majority of tourists were from Western Europe and Australia. Today, the majority are from Russia and, increasingly, China.

Sadly, the Chinese tend to come on fully organised tours where they are whisked from one large restaurant to another, then to a mega jewellery store or souvenir emporium and, sadly, often animal-based tourism attractions such as Phuket Fantasea, the shocking Phuket Zoo, Tiger Kingdom, and the dolphin show.

Many of the places the tourists are taken to are Chinese-owned, so the local people are benefitting little from them. Hopefully, future generations of Chinese will become more independent and more aware of the suffering that goes on in providing such entertainment, although Westerners are as bad. I have got into trouble on more than one occasion lecturing tourists paying to have their photos taken with endangered species. However, back in 1996 we were also oblivious to all of this.

Beaches in Thailand are all owned by the king and are open to everyone. Try telling that to the local beach-chair operator or luxury hotel. In 1996, you could walk along the beach and would find occasional restaurants, but also plenty of places where locals could be seen fishing.

Fast forward twenty years and you would be lucky to find any decent beach not completely taken over by what were essentially illegal restaurants and bars. Much of it was controlled by a local mafia, and the majority of beaches were eyesores, although the owners would at least keep their patch of sand clean, even if the land behind resembled a garbage dump.

Step forward the government, who announced a clean-up. All restaurants and chair operators etc. had to go or their premises would be bulldozed into submission. Initially on some beaches, including the ones near us, they did just that and it was wonderful to see the beaches looking natural again and local people being able to enjoy them. But the reality is that Phuket is a tourist destination, and returning tourists were shocked to find their favourite beach restaurant now a pile of rubble. Having no beach chair on which to lounge on and have the occasional massage and drink brought to you, so many vowed never to return.

There has to be a middle ground surely: areas set aside for restaurants and bars and other areas left to nature.

Today, some restaurants and upmarket beach bars are allowed to operate on the beach, while those that were run by locals are not allowed. Probably a case of who you know and how much you can pay, sadly.

In other areas, landowners who own land behind the beaches are fencing it off and denying access through it to the beach. Signs proclaiming the land for sale at prices only the largest companies can afford are everywhere.

I foresee a day when the only way you will be able to enjoy a holiday on one of Phuket's beaches is if you can afford to stay in a hotel set on it.

That, of course, is precisely what we were doing now. As first-time visitors to Thailand we were swept away by the beauty of its tropical landscape; the exotic east was certainly here.

A beautiful hotel on a beautiful bay with fresh seafood restaurants a short stroll along the beach where you could enjoy fabulous sunsets. Animal abuse? Stray dogs and cats? We, like most tourists, were oblivious to it, and the hotel ensured our visit would not be disturbed by any stray dog daring to show itself in their grounds.

Our one and only trip ever to the Phi Phi islands, other than a trip John made to help the cats and kittens after the tsunami, found an island with just a few beach bungalows dotting the shore. A completely different picture to the island today.

Our favourite trip was in John Gray's sea canoe. He had discovered the hongs (in effect lagoons in the middle of limestone islands), which could only be accessed by a canoe paddled by a guide through tunnels only reachable at low tide.

It was like entering a forgotten world. The islands were in the fabulous landscape of Phang Nga Bay, and John Gray ran the original sea canoe trips, which were the best trip on the island.

Today, the number of companies mean you have to queue to get in to the islands, and these companies generally show little respect for the environment. Fortunately, you can still go out in the afternoon and evening with John Gray when all the others have gone home. Even I, who am not keen on boats, loved this trip.

Not surprisingly, the days leading up to our wedding flew by, and before we knew it the great day arrived. The hotel staff were brilliant. I had the services of two members of staff to help me get ready. At the appointed time we began the procession from our room to the foyer with traditional musicians leading the way and followed by staff in traditional dress, including the young son and daughter of our maid, who looked very smart and proud.

With camera flashes going off along the route and guests clapping, I felt more like a film star than just Gill from Leeds.

In the foyer, flower arches, beautiful floral displays, and a beautiful huge ice carving of two doves helped to transform it. Rows of chairs were filled with hotel guests from the UK that the hotel had invited, and in front of us was a low table with various bowls and flowers, behind which sat four monks.

At the back of the room were two ladies in uniform who were the official registrars. The actual ceremony took around half an hour. We didn't understand a word of what was being chanted, but our Thai assistants guided us through what to do and say.

The ceremony included pouring water on to each other's hands, placing joined garlands of flowers on our heads, and painting marks on our foreheads. I couldn't contain a laugh when the head monk, who, as part of the ceremony, had a small brush-like implement which he dipped in water and in effect anointed us with it, also decided to shower people standing behind him, who he obviously thought were not showing enough respect for proceedings.

I'm not sure if it is part of Thai tradition, but we were able to exchange rings and kisses at the end of the ceremony. Wedding ceremonies always take place in the morning so the monks have time to eat before their midday curfew, after which they are not allowed to eat.

Once the monks had left with their food, we went to sign the register and were given our original wedding certificate, which was promptly whisked off to be taken to an official translation office. Although to my knowledge nobody actually pronounced us man and wife, I was assured we were now officially married.

Following the ceremony, the hotel produced a beautiful cake and bottles of champagne for ourselves and the guests.

I passed on the cake, but the champagne was gratefully received. After that, it was out into the grounds for official photos at various locations. The photographer was probably not the greatest, but as a wedding present, John's eldest son's then girlfriend and now wife, who is an award-winning wedding photographer, recreated the scene in our garden at home and took some beautiful photos for us.

Finally, somewhat sweaty, although we had been followed around by two maids who repeatedly mopped our brows, we were taken back to our room only to find everything had been moved to a nearby suite. The rooms again were full of flowers with roses draped all around the bed and petals forming the shape of a heart on the bed itself. When it comes to arts and crafts, the Thai really are so talented. We chilled out for a time and that evening ate dinner at a traditional Thai banquet at the hotel's restaurant, which overlooked one of the lagoons. Well, I had wanted a special day and it truly was wonderful.

Neither John nor I are big breakfast eaters. We had been told we would have breakfast served in our room, but imagine our surprise the next day when three chefs arrived along with waiters with mobile cookers into the living room area of the suite. How the other half live.

Not wanting to disappoint the chefs, we valiantly ordered something from each of them and battled through the food.

The following day, we completed one more ceremony in the hotel grounds. We were invited to plant a love tree. We were only the second couple to marry at the hotel so ours was tree number two. Twenty years later, I am happy to report that among the now dozens of little wooden plaques marking the dates of weddings, ours was still surviving, though as they are picked up and re-varnished regularly I doubt very much it is the same tree. Still it's a nice touch. [When John returned in 2018 he was unable to find it].

Many people consider marriage an outdated and meaningless institution, especially when so many end in divorce. Maybe it is, but I see it as an act of commitment, a public declaration of love, and certainly at the time it is made I assume everybody feels that way. Although John and I never did it, I fully approve of those couples who decide to reaffirm their vows after years of marriage.

Our holiday was not quite over yet. We had one more day and night at the Dusit Laguna before one final trip to another Dusit-managed hotel for our honeymoon.

The Rayavadee was in Krabi province, and we would spend our final four nights there. It was only accessible by boat, and after a two-hour drive we boarded a launch which took us to this beautifully situated resort.

We had our own private two-storey villa overlooking the small limestone islands and pinnacles in Krabi Bay, which is just an extension of Phang Nga Bay.

It was stunning, although some may say an odd choice for somebody who does not like water, but I knew John would love it and the snorkelling was amazing, he told me.

On one occasion, while wearing a life-jacket, I did actually trust him to hold me, and with mask and snorkel attached I put my face in the water. It was beautiful but not enough to tempt me to prolong the experience any more than necessary.

John could do the snorkelling and I would watch from the beach. I can actually swim and am happy to go in a pool so long as nobody is splashing water around me. For somebody who is not afraid of anything much, it seems odd that I hate water on my face, but I suppose most people have something they are irrationally frightened of.

Our trip of a lifetime was coming to an end. Exactly a month after we departed from a cold and wintry UK, we would be returning to hopefully find spring on its way. Was it worth it? One hundred percent yes.

I had saved up for it, and the memories, particularly our wedding day, would remain with me for the rest of my life.

I had fulfilled a dream for the man I loved and, unknowingly at the time, taken another step on what was a pre-destined journey, if you believe my fortune-teller.

What's more, when I see how much people spend just on a wedding day alone these days, we actually had the experience of a lifetime on the cheap.

I had fallen in love with Thailand, and although holidays can and do give a false picture of a destination and are escapes from everyday reality, I really felt at home here.

So many Thais tell me that in a previous life I must have been Thai. As I would with all subsequent holidays, I shed a few tears as our plane took off, little knowing that one day I would not be leaving and this place would become my home.

We arrived in London early morning on 20 March and had a connecting flight to Leeds.

The weather at home lived up to its reputation and there was no sign of spring. As our plane approached Leeds and Bradford Airport, the captain announced it was cold and windy and four degrees. John and I grimaced at each other as we recalled the sun-drenched tropical beach we had just left behind.

Just Gill

# The Wilderness Years

I have called this chapter 'The Wilderness Years', (directly stealing from Winston Churchill's book and TV series). Not to imply that nothing happened in this period, as quite the opposite is true, but it bridges that gap between our first visit to Thailand and finally moving there seven years later and what happened then – which is, of course, the main point of this book.

I was thirty-seven years old when I married John, who was forty-six. Traditionally, John had another nineteen years to go before he reached retirement age, although even then he had plans to retire early.

I was now officially on the scrap heap. I had loved my job and, to be truthful, was quite bitter that the bank had deemed me not physically fit enough to work but refused to accept that this had anything to do with them, or rather the work that I had been doing for them for the past twenty years.

The government doctors deemed me disabled and awarded me a pension, which I have never felt guilty about accepting. I abhor scroungers. There is no doubt, as I had noticed in Thailand, that when the weather was warm I could use my arms and hands quite well. But during the winter months I was severely restricted and suffered a lot of pain. I remember my own doctor telling me on one occasion that the best thing I could do was move to the tropics.

I became a full-time housewife looking after John and our 'babies'. A year after Crystal passed, I got the first of two Burmese kittens who we called Suai (Thai for beautiful) and a year later a second called Sanuk (Thai for good luck). It was good to have cats around again.

My pension, albeit quite small, did at least give me some feeling of independence and of contributing. Although John always told me it made no difference to him and he would much rather me be at home, I did hate not having full independence.

Our walks and theatre trips, and most importantly our days in, all continued, and we were to go back to Asia at least once a year and on occasion squeezed in an extra trip to Phuket during the low season, when bargains could be had.

Despite my physical issues, these wilderness years were the happiest of my life so far. I was with somebody who I loved and who loved me. We did have our rows as all couples do, and there has been more than one broken door or window pane as when I do lose it, like John, I really do lose it. The only difference is that my fuse is far shorter than his! They were always short-lived, though, and whatever the pretext, they were always about my insecurities and John's lack of understanding of them.

Following Johnathan's rejection of my body I had become bulimic, and this continued for years into my marriage to John before I was finally able to accept that he loved me for who I was and if he was staying with me despite my various health problems, then my body was not something I need worry about.

Everything else was perfect. We don't always agree on everything, and nobody likes to admit they are wrong. As far as John was concerned, he was always right, but then so was I, so how could he be? We are so alike in many ways, yet so different in others. Fortunately, our love for animals and our hatred of their abuse is one where we are absolutely at one.

One area where we are not alike is what we believe in spiritually. Despite John's flirtation with the Mormon Church, neither of us were religious, but I do believe in spirits, and during this period of my life I became more involved.

I learned how to use crystals and Tarot cards and even divining rods. I was to meet the spirit of my natural father via a medium and see my guardian angel. Rubbish? You believe what you want to. John, of course, does not believe in such things. For him, everything has to have a rational explanation, though even he could not work out how he could hide one of my crystals anywhere he liked in the house, and within a minute or two I would always find it with my divining rods.

In the same way, I could tell any pregnant woman the sex of her child by using a crystal as a pendulum. If it swung one way it was a boy; the other way, a girl – and it was never wrong.

I gave it up after we moved to Thailand as I no longer had time to practise it, but my crystals and Tarot cards always remained under my pillow. Bottom line is, just because you don't understand something doesn't make it wrong. How much intolerance in this world would be avoided if people would accept that?

We had some fabulous weekends, and I could write a travel guide on where to stay in the Yorkshire Dales and the North Yorkshire Moors national parks. We always stayed in dog-friendly pubs and discovered some great ones.

One that shall remain nameless has long since changed hands, but when we used to stay there, the landlord, like most in those days in these sorts of areas, totally ignored licensing laws, and on more than one occasion would stagger home to his own house a few hundred yards away and leave us with the keys, which was very dangerous!

On one occasion, John's sons stayed with us there and we were still enjoying ourselves when the landlord came back in the morning. Needless to say, John had given up hours earlier – a party animal he is not! Me? If I am enjoying myself I don't want it to end, and John has dragged a reluctant me off on more occasions than I can remember.

His hobby at this time was marine aquariums, natural reef tanks in particular. On our next trip to Thailand, he took up diving, and this was to lead to his first moral dilemma regarding animal welfare.

He already knew that virtually all marine fish and invertebrates sold in the aquarium industry were wild caught. What he hadn't realised was the destruction being caused as a result. Although there were some reputable companies around who trained local people on how to catch fish with hand nets, the use of cyanide and even dynamiting reefs to catch fish led to most dying or being so badly affected that they did not live long once caught.

He had learned that hard corals and anemones were notoriously difficult to keep alive longer than a few months, and although some species of coral are now being successfully grown in captivity, most did not survive more than a few months in a closed aquarium system.

It was not long before he abandoned his aquarium and started campaigning for an end to the importing of coral, which was collected by hacking lumps off reefs that had taken hundreds of years to grow.

Just like wild animals in tourist attractions, these creatures should be left alone in their natural habitat to be observed there, providing it is done with care. Probably not for the last time in this book, I will state here and now that if God *did* create this planet, then the only mistake he made was putting us humans here.

John also got involved with a small organisation called Pet Watch and did some investigating for them. One case, strangely, involved dog meat.

A man in Leeds had been heard bragging that he was catching dogs on the housing estate where he lived, killing them, and storing them in a freezer. Once he had enough he would drive them to London and sell them to Korean restaurants there.

In the event, John never found any evidence and believed the guy was probably making it up, but he only had limited time to watch him so who knows?

Another case involved the RSPCA and local vets disposing of euthanised dogs and cats to a company in Lancashire, who would skin the animals and sell the pelts to Germany for use in toys and fun furs. In those days, the RSPCA were responsible for taking in abandoned and stray animals, and if not claimed or adopted within ten days, they were euthanised.

Although not illegal, it did raise moral issues, and subsequently the RSPCA started to spray-paint the coats of animals it euthanised. Local vets justified it by pointing out that owners could take the animal home and bury it themselves.

John's view, with which I fully agreed, was that if, for example, an elderly lady paid a vet to put her cat to sleep, then it was not ethical to pass the carcass on to a company knowing its pelt would be used to make a toy or a fur clothing item without telling the lady first.

What angered John most about the RSPCA involvement is that he had witnessed first-hand dozens of dead dogs and cats being thrown on to the company's truck each week at the Leeds branch off Burley Road, but had also met a car dealer in Leeds who was saving as many dogs as he could from the RSPCA death row and then successfully rehoming them.

John discovered the car dealer had to pay £30 per dog to save them, whereas in reality he was saving the RSPCA the cost of paying a vet to come and euthanise them. That is not to say that the RSPCA don't do some wonderful work, but that policy was certainly a stain on their reputation in those days.

On holiday, we would generally visit somewhere new for a few days and then finish off with ten days relaxing in Phuket. During this time, I would keep journals of our holidays, entering our thoughts and experiences. John would contribute under sufferance, but I hope they will bring back happy memories for him in the future.

Our first holiday after our marriage started off in Vietnam, a country which, much later, was to have an important part to play in the future of Soi Dog.

In 1997, tourism was still in its infancy. We visited Saigon, Danang, Hue, and Hanoi. We had heard that northerners ate dog meat, but thankfully never saw any sign of it or I would likely have ended up being arrested.

Vietnam is a beautiful country, but even twenty-five years after the war, the differences were very evident. Saigon had an entrepreneurial feel to it. The city was buzzing and alive. At night, thousands of people would simply promenade around the main streets on motorcycles or on foot. They didn't seem to be going anywhere, but were just happy to be out and alive.

By contrast, Hanoi at that time seemed very austere and the people glum. Even though they had been victorious in the war, the people there did not seem as alive and happy as their southern cousins. The Central Highlands were beautiful. Hoi An was already a World Heritage Site, but it and Danang were still years away from becoming the centre of the Vietnamese tourism boom.

Hue still showed the ravages of war, and as white-faced foreigners we were still a curiosity to the locals.

It was not the best trip for me. I got kicked in the eye accidentally while crawling through the Chu Chi tunnels by another tourist, and then got suspected food poisoning resulting in chronic diarrhoea when in the Central Highlands.

The hotel in Hue called a doctor, which was certainly an experience. He diagnosed appendicitis, which it clearly was not, and prescribed various pills together with his bill, which was probably a week's normal salary, and disappeared.

When we reached Hanoi our guide stopped off at a local herbalist, told me 'take these', and gave me tablets, which he refused payment for. Within a few hours the symptoms had gone.

That is a good lesson for anybody visiting out-of-the-way places in Asia. The local pharmacists are often better than the local doctors for treating common ailments.

The only other holiday experience to mention outside of Phuket is Malaysian Borneo. We visited twice for a few days, once to Sabah and once to Sarawak.

It is the Sabah experience that will remain with me. Initially, we stayed just outside Kota Kinabalu, overlooking the sea. While John went off diving, I took a trip up the lower slopes of Mount Kinabalu to see orchids, which had become another passion of mine.

John had built me a large greenhouse, and I had become friends with the owners of a local orchid nursery and would help them at shows in return for plants.

In Malaysia and Thailand I would buy small plants for next to nothing and carefully wrap them and take them home. Whether this was strictly legal I have no idea, but nobody ever queried it.

We then decided to take a short flight to the eastern side of the island and the town of Sandakan. This was the gateway to the world-famous dive site of Sipadan, but John would have to forego that pleasure, as the point of this trip was to see a particular type of marine creature that did not involve diving and also visit the orangutan sanctuary.

The flight made it only too painfully obvious why these great apes, who are genetically very close to ourselves, are struggling to survive. Below us, the rivers were brown, and you could actually see brown soil spreading into the sea as we took off.

The reason was clear to see. Great swathes of rainforest had been cleared away by man wherever you looked, taking with it the home of these beautiful animals. I will say it again: the only thing that needs removing from this planet is us.

Before we saw the orangutans, though, we had booked an overnight visit to Selangan, otherwise known as Turtle Island. Note there are many places that call themselves Turtle Island that are nothing more than tourist traps, and nothing to do with turtle conservation.

This place was not one of them, and I hope it is the same today. Below are extracts from my diary written at the time:

10 am. We are in the bus to the harbour, our guide is called Alvin. Total journey time 1 hour 30 minutes. 10:12 and we are on a small speedboat, I already have my life jacket on – why do I let myself in for these things? It's going to be an hour and a half of hell. We have been going now for 40 minutes, the clouds in the sky are wonderful, they look superimposed. When we set off we passed lots of Sea Gypsy houses and the amount of rubbish in the sea was just terrible, and in fact we had to stop at one point to unravel a plastic bag from the propeller, guess who did not like that one bit!

I suppose years ago the garbage would all have been biodegradable and food for fish, all this plastic is just killing the seas. Alvin tells us that the Philippines are just 3 kilometres away from Turtle Island so armed marines patrol it to protect the turtles and their eggs from poachers. We will stop at another island for lunch and then 30 minutes later reach Turtle Island.

I know I've mentioned it before but the more I look at the clouds the more remarkable and mystical they become. I've never seen clouds like them, so I've just taken three shots of them though how they will turn out when the boat is moving about I don't know. . . we'll see. J has just seen a turtle swimming at the surface in the direction of Turtle Island. You never know maybe we'll see her tonight.

2:05pm We are on the island and have filled out a registration form each. We have been allocated room B8. There are quite a few other people here already and we have been told it can accommodate 38 tourists a day. We are all moved in and it is not as basic as I thought it would be. We have a fridge in our room with two bottles of water (small) in it so it's good I've brought some of my own.

We will meet at 6:55 pm at the cafeteria, eat and then simply wait for the turtles. We could have to wait until 3am, last night it was 8:30am, you never know but this is one place where turtles come and lay eggs virtually every night of the year. I don't care what time it is so long as it is not one of those rare nights when they don't appear at all. I'm in the shade on the beach now and J has gone off snorkel and flippers in hand. I'm just going to lay back and relax and you never know I may get some shut eye. It is so peaceful and I can see J swimming and oh yes I forgot to mention that on the way from the cafeteria we saw a large monitor lizard, what a haven, no wonder the turtles use it. Just the sound of the sea, birds and insects. I can see six small islands and all of them are part of the national park but you can only stay on this one.

J came back for a cig and sunbathe for 20 minutes before going back with camera and snorkel. I decided to go for a cool off in the shallows and J saw me and tried to persuade me to go for a snorkel but no life jacket, no snorkel. On the way back I saw a poor dead baby turtle being eaten by ants, poor thing only had one flipper left. At 4pm we took everything back to the chalet and set off to walk all the way round the island. It was lovely and took only half an hour which shows how small it is.

We bought some beers from the cafeteria and stopped off at the hatchery to take some photos. We kept hearing rustles in the undergrowth but whatever it was too quick to be spotted.

We then got showered. Only cold water but that was so, so, so welcome and yet another pleasant surprise was that it was fresh water not as we had been led to believe salt. Each chalet has aircon but not turned on until 6pm, but they also have a fan in each room. There is in effect a curfew at 6pm. You can only use the footpath between the chalet and the cafeteria, not take any photos after 6pm. There are a lot of rules some of which seem over the top such as no camcording at any time but others are all there to protect the turtles.

We did not see any armed guards on our walk and it is now 5:50pm and we'll be setting off to meet Alvin at 6:50pm. We are having a welcome beer and ciggy under the fan on our verandah. I do hope we get to see a turtle tonight, but whatever as I said to J earlier we really are the luckiest, and if we do see a turtle the most privileged people I know, especially when you consider how much in love we are who could ask for more? No one!

I've just seen a man running down towards the hatchery. First thought turtle, so up we jumped and followed. At the hatchery a monitor lizard had got in and was after his evening meal. The lads who work there had sticks and were trying to get him out. He was not a happy lizard and boy, oh boy can they thrash about. His tail made a real whip crack as he flicked it with all his might. It can break a man's leg so they needed to be careful. I must admit I felt for him, he was being prodded to try and get him to the low part of the fence and he was obviously frightened. After a few minutes one of the lads got a branch and managed to oik him out. He went scuttling off into the undergrowth. I hope it's a sign of things to come this evening as in lots of things to see. Now 6:10pm so no more photos.

There has just been a flash of lightning in the sky and J says another has just happened. Well we have our Cling Film macs so who cares. 6:45pm and walking to the cafeteria, we see lots and lots of very large fruit bats. It's still lightning and lightening up the whole sky. I've just said to John what a couple of days it's going to be and it's the nearest I'll come to imitating David Attenborough.

7:45pm and dinner is over, J didn't enjoy. I enjoyed the fish but have just been as sick as a dog. Outside parts of the beach are lit up and someone is walking around with a torch. The sky is still being lit up by lightning, but there is no cloud above and the stars are absolutely amazing. They seem so much closer here and you can feel you can reach out and touch them. A shooting star has just passed by – oh I do feel it is going to be one magical evening. 8:20pm and we have just finished our briefing. We have to wait here until a turtle comes up and starts to lay. We are then called and can watch the laying and feel the eggs which are soft. They start to mate when they are 20 years old and each female is mated by up to six males. She comes up to lay her eggs in batches. They are taken away by the staff and put in the hatchery.

The gestation period is 49 days/7 weeks. They are released at night to ensure the least number of predators are about. Once she has finished laying, the wardens measure her and tag her. Even though she knows her eggs are gone, her instincts still tell her to cover the nest. She digs the nest which is like a crater to her own height with all four fins, then using the back ones only, she digs the egg chamber. Only if the sand conditions are right and there are no obstructions will she drop the eggs. It can take from two-seven hours to complete. If she gets tired she will abort her mission. Because turtles are laying every night eggs are also hatching every day. We will be given a baby to hold before we release them. They don't tag the babies as they are too small and soft. Out of every 2,000 released only six pairs will survive to maturity. We saw some craters on the beach today which are phantom craters, the sand which came out of them is the sand used to cover the nest thus creating a diversion from the eggs.

J said the stars have disappeared, or as he literally put it the sky has disappeared so it must have clouded over. Turtles only lay eggs every three-four years and nobody knows how long they live for. Turtle eggs have six times more cholesterol than hen's eggs and no matter how long you boil them for they never go hard both inside and out.

Alvin has said he's our guide for the Orangutans tomorrow as well so that makes things easier. Provided we are not still up at 6am he will give us a knock and we have to meet here at 6:30pm for breakfast with our luggage to leave at 7am prompt for the 90 minute return journey.

10pm and no turtles. Alvin has only had two nights since 1977 when not one has come. Each fully grown turtle weighs between 120 and 160 kilos, the females being larger than the males. The males have longer tails, they have lungs and can stay under water for 30 minutes before they have to surface and breathe again.

The green turtles (the ones we are waiting to see) are herbivorous whereas the hornbills are carnivores and eat jelly fish, crabs, fish etc. Alvin reckons it will be a minimum of two hours before anything happens. This is because the tide is very low at the moment. The wind has started to get up – rain? Only time will tell for both.

10:10pm and they have decided to release the baby turtles. A blue bucket arrives with 62 babies in it. We were each given one to hold and they are about the size of a matchbox with flippers approximately twice the length of an adult in relation to their size. They start the action of swimming straight away. Their strength in relation to their size is incredible, so so so strong. If the statistics are correct then at best only one of them will survive.

I know they have a far better chance this way as if left to nature many would never even reach the sea or even hatch. None the less it brought tears to my eyes and I asked the spirits if possible that they can help them on their way, especially mine who I have named Herman – Lord knows why, he just is.

It was a wonderful sight to see them instinctively go to the water and push their way in and then bob up and down like little corks. Just as nature can be cruel, she can also create miracles and wonderful spectacles.

I'll never forget that little body in my hand and the mass exodus as long as I live. I just feel very emotional and very, very privileged. 10:50pm and the wait for an expectant mum continues, the heavens have opened and it's raining turtles, well it seems more apt than cats and dogs. Some people have given up and gone to bed. Midnight and no turtles. J is trying to sleep. He went back to the chalet to take his eyes out, (contact lenses) and brought me back some crisps which were very welcome. We are down to 10 people now and then at 12:15 we get the call; 'she's landed'.

We all jumped up like our bums were on fire. Off we ran following the ranger. She was at the top of the beach and was already laying her eggs. The metal pole we saw the rangers carrying is used to hold up one of her back flippers so we and importantly the ranger can see the eggs.

7:00am We are on the boat. I did not have time to finish last night as we went to bed at 1:15 am. We watched as egg after egg dropped. All were lubricated with a clear sticky fluid. We were given an egg to hold, they were white and perfectly round and although not soft soft, they had a slight give to them. After 10 minutes or so she finished laying but carried on straining for a minute or two. The ranger then removed the sand from her shell and measured her; 96cms long and 83cms wide. She had been here before as was already tagged.

They counted 96 eggs, not bad in one lay. In the wild if not disturbed around 80-90% hatch but doing it this way 65-70% will hatch, this is due to this very short disturbance and movement of the eggs, but on the plus side they can guarantee that 100% of the hatchlings reach the sea.

The mother then started to cover the nest with her back fins. The movement was like a car's windscreen wipers and it did not take long to cover the actual nest hole. We then left her to fill in the crater and create a 'dummy' nest as it can take anything from two to five hours to complete.

We then rushed to the hatchery where a hole was dug approximately 80cms deep, the eggs were placed in and covered and then a cylinder of green mesh was placed around approximately 18inches high to stop the babies escaping when they do hatch. It takes seven weeks for them to hatch and can take up to two days for them to reach the surface and they are released that night.

A wooden marker is placed above each nest and in this case it was labelled 20-3-99, (Date they were laid), 96E (96 eggs) and number 687 (The 687th nest that year).

We then went back to our chalet and had a drink and cig with Alvin who told us that each turtle has to eat half its own bodyweight in food every day. Just before our turtle came up another one came up near the cafeteria side of the beach hut, but she aborted her lay for some reason.

By this time it was 1:15am so as we had to be up at 6:00 am it was off to bed. All I can say is that I would not have missed this for the world. It was a wonderful sight and an amazing experience and I've said it before and will say it again I feel honoured and privileged to have been one of the few people lucky enough to have witnessed such a miracle of nature.

I really feel inadequate in my description of my feelings, it was just awesome. She was so so beautiful, I never thought I would see anything like it. So I went to bed with warm thoughts and once again felt quite emotional thinking about Herman and all the other babies released. I shed a couple of tears; not sad tears not happy tears just tears of wonderment.

5:50am Woke up and two minutes later Alvin was knocking at the door with our wakeup call. So dressed, packed and off to the cafeteria for breakfast. We stopped at the hatchery to see if any more nests had been dug and yes six more so seven successful lays last night.

John went over to where our turtle had laid her eggs and there were lots of other tracks so appears that all the lays had happened on the same stretch. We then had breakfast and I went to have a look at her nest and all the other tracks that came out of the sea were still very clear. Some were straight and were going over small obstacles such as logs and some were zig-zag.

On the way back we passed two large barges being towed by a tug, each barge laden with huge logs, as J has just said; 'another bit of rainforest gone'. We brought up with Alvin about the posters stating it only takes a little bit of plastic to kill a turtle as they think it is a jelly fish. We see plastic floating everywhere as well as being washed up on the island.

The rangers clear it away but obviously it's a losing battle. Most of it in this area comes from the stilt houses on the sea shore at Sandukan. I couldn't believe it but millionaires live there and

J has read that Sandukan used to have the largest number of millionaires per capita in the world. Probably before the war and probably through logging.

It's now onto orangutans at Sepilok.

There are 78 orangutans at the centre which started in 1964. It covers 64 square kilometers. Alvin is telling us all about them. I can't possibly write it all down so hopefully I'll get some info at the centre. Each male matures at aged 9-10 years and females at 7-8. They make a new bed each day and use it as an umbrella as well. They live alone and females only give birth three-four times in their lifetime. The baby stays with mum until it's five years old. There is the Sumatran Orangutan and the Borneo Orangutan. Once we had signed in we went straight to feeding platform A.

Area A is a halfway house and when the orangutans no longer come to be fed then they are taken to Area B. In Area A they are fed bananas and milk twice a day to encourage them to look for their own food. Bananas and milk get boring when you have them every day. It can take a long time to happen though, years and years.

We saw a male and a female both around six-seven years old and both making nests. As it got nearer feeding time they came down from the trees and started walking about among us, real show offs. They are very close as both were orphaned at the same time. Then another male of a similar age appeared. Talk about snap happy with the camera. They can touch you but you are not allowed to touch them. Alvin then spotted a mum with her 12-15 month old baby high in the trees nearby.

9:55am She started to move down as feeding is at 10. Another male followed close behind approximately 8-9 years old. The ranger came with buckets of bananas and milk. There were also a lot of Macac monkeys around which can be nasty. One adult got hold of someone's tripod and began shaking it about with great force. It was actually quite amusing to watch them darting in and out pinching bananas. When the mum came down she looked large, but once she sat down (Asian style squat – bum one inch off the floor) she looked quite small.

As the feeding went on, the younger ones started playing with their food, spurting out milk and pouring it over themselves. Mum gave her baby a banana to eat and to say the baby was over a year old it did seem small, but I suppose they grow similar to us.

When new ones arrive at the centre they have to go into quarantine for six months. As they carry 96.8% of our genes they are also susceptible to our diseases, typhoid, polio and the most common; malaria.

It was wonderful to see them perform, if perform is the right word, as they are natural show-offs. It wasn't quite the total real thing of last night but the next best thing. We then walked back to the centre as they disappear once feeding is over. We were shown a video of the history of the centre, which was both happy and sad and also how some of the orangutans came to be there.

One male approximately nine years old had been raiding a homestead that had been claimed from HIS home the forest. So they had chained him up and beaten him and used a whip which had caused his bottom lip to be almost ripped off. Terrible.

Another was a baby found as a pet in a family home. He was taken and the family fined, (not enough), but had they been trading that would have meant a prison sentence. A baby orangutan can fetch 10,000$ on the black market.

We then went into the gift shop but bought nothing as nothing to buy – what a surprise. We had seen signs about their adoption (sponsorship) programme but when we enquired how to do it nobody seemed to know. It was not a surprise to learn they are short of funds. They charge only 10RM to get in which was about £1.60p, so I left 50RM in the donation box.

I do hope they are better organised these days.

I shall not bore you with the details of our holidays, but clearly what we saw on our holidays in Thailand and one incident in particular, was what was drove us to move there and try to do something to change the lives of those poor dogs.

Like most holidaymakers, days were spent in the confines of our touristy 'luxury' hotel, sunbathing on the grass lawn just outside our room fronting onto the beach, with occasional swims when it got too hot.

Evenings were spent wining and dining at bars and restaurants within walking distance of the hotel -- you didn't see many dogs around, the hotels made sure of that. It was only when we went to the local market I became aware of all the skinny dogs, often with no fur and looking diseased, that we caught a glimpse of what lay behind this paradise. At the local market we would buy some barbecued chicken and (much to the amusement of the locals) feed this to the dogs, who would snatch it from your hand and scuttle off under a stall to eat it as if it was the first meal they had had in days.

I imagine the locals thought we were 'crazy *farangs*' spending money on chicken and then giving it to the dogs. As we spent further holidays here, we also began to explore more and would hire a car. The dogs were everywhere, thousands of them. On one visit, we met an American woman, Eve Lentz, who lived not far from our hotel. Eve and some like-minded friends had started a group caring for dogs at some of the Phuket's many temples.

Eve looked after three temples in the area where we stayed. She would feed the dogs, give them first aid, as well as tick and flea treatment, and was slowly getting them sterilised at local vets. Eve's husband was the head chef at a luxurious resort and Eve got the left-over meat and fish from the hotel, which usually went to pig farms and then supplement this with dried dog food which she would buy. The temples had dozens of dogs and cats, and we discovered that they were also traditional dumping grounds for many unwanted puppies and kittens. It was believed that the monks would look after them, and although there were some monks who clearly cared and shared food with them; these animals were mostly tolerated rather than wanted.

It was on a holiday in March 1998 that we met the dog that was to change everything.

Naga (I named him after a mythical Thai dragon-like creature), was the driving force behind us being determined to help Thai stray dogs. It was the habit of the hotel to have weekly early evening cocktail parties for returning guests and that is surprisingly where we first met Naga. The following are extracts from my diary:

> At the cocktail parry there were an English couple and an American couple. The English couple were the ones we'd seen walking with the white dog who was with them now. The lady told us she had named the dog Sandy Beach, (their American friends had named him Fleabag). He had been 'adopted' by them but they are going home tomorrow and could we look out for him?
>
> She told us he had been passed on to her by a Spanish/Belgian/Swiss couple, (the story changed as the evening wore on), he had had a hole in his head seen to by a local vet. He also had a zig-zag scar running from his ear which John reckoned was where a vet had stitched it at some point. They also said the management were trying to get rid of him? So tomorrow I am going to call the vets we read about in the paper to see if we can't do something to help him. I would love to take him home but I could not bear to see him in six months quarantine – he's a free sprit and I think

it would be just terrible for him. . .

John has been talking to one of the waitresses and she has written down for me where I can get a dog collar and lead – Robinson's department store in Phuket Town 1st. Floor.

[Back then there were no pet stores like there are now]. We left at 11pm and just near the room Naga (Sandy) as I have named him appeared and followed me to our door but he was in front of me and the most amazing, wonderful thing happened; he stopped at our room door before me. He came in and refused a drink and biscuit but sniffed the whole room. I tried to film him but don't think it will come out well. John is shagged and Naga has gone walkabout. John in bed at 11:45 and now 12:15 and no Naga. Requested a wake up call for 8am as John diving me Phuket Town. . .

Up at 6am and John at 8am with the call. My mind is in a quandary over Naga. I just don't know what to do for the best. Tried to call the vets and got through at 9:30. Girl did not speak English but she kept saying English 11, so I'll phone back at 11 from Phuket Town. I am going to walk through the gardens to get the bus to see if I can see Naga. Left room at 9:50, went through gardens and no sign of Naga. Went and saw the general manager and he assured me he'd told the personnel manager last night to take him to a temple for the monks to look after and that he would be OK. So, as he seemed genuine I think we can be assured that Naga is now with the monks as he said to me what a lovely friendly dog he was. . .

I got back 11:50am. I went to find the personnel manager to find out about Naga as John had suggested renting a car and going to see him and making a donation to the temple. He made a phone call and told me that the security guards said they had taken him to a village up by the bridge which connects Phuket to the mainland and dumped him at a food stall or café where they thought he'd be given scraps. I asked if anyone was looking after him?

The answer – No.

So he had definitely not gone to a temple? – Correct. My blood is boiling: 'I assure you he will be taken to a temple and looked after by the monks'. The bloody lying bastard. Wait 'til I see him! I made him quite aware that I would see to him and his welfare, but no I foolishly believed this man's lies. I want to smack him around the head and make him sing soprano. Enough! I am so so so angry and upset, first the Gibbons' story and now I learn the truth about poor Naga. Why did I believe him? . . .

In bed now and having a ciggy and we're talking about Naga. Oh I wish I knew what to do for the best. The quarantine, our other animals, J's mum if she stayed. If he came to the UK he is used to being free so what would six months in a cage do to him, especially after this week's episode of being caught, bagged up, and then dumped? Oh I am going to write a stinker of a letter not only to the general manager but to the CEO of the hotel group. If I see him as I said earlier, I'll let sentiment rule my head. The temple seems the best thing as John said to be sensible. Well its 12:30 and we're off to sleep- thoughts of Naga and thoughts of leaving Thailand running through my head – oh for a Lottery win and we could really do wonders. A dog and cat sanctuary here maybe? Wouldn't it be wonderful? The suffering we could end and to educate people about spaying etc. Dreams can come true can't they? Oh well as John said he will be surprised if he can even find Naga.'

Up at 8:45am and we are having our coffee outside discussing Naga. John is going to hire a car for a few hours as he thinks it will be easier than hiring a taxi. First we will go and see the manager and find out the name of the village and to put in our formal complaint. John is going to say how angry we are and how upset I am. He now has to drive around for the last day of our holiday to try and find Naga to keep me happy.

If he does find him he is going to take him to the vets and pay for him to be checked over and kept for a few days. You never know we may end up with him after all!

The manager is still in Bangkok and won't be back until after we have gone. What a surprise. His Thai deputy listens to us and made some phone calls and fortunately was able to find out the name of the village so at 10:15 John's off on his pursuit, oh I hope he finds him.

The Thai manager does not say much which is the Thai way, but it does leave Westerners infuriated. I'm still going to write and play merry hell! I went to get some last minute shopping and then I'm going to pack. Please John, please take care and find him. I love you, you're wonderful.

I finished packing at 1pm and two minutes later John walked in.

No luck, Naga not to be seen anywhere. He found the school quarter of a mile past the line of food stalls along the beach. John said it was very quiet, not many people and the roads were dead. From what the manager said it is the place where Naga was dumped. John said it was a nice place and I said you're not just saying that for my benefit are you? No was the reply. I believed him. Well there's nothing more we can do. I love John so much for doing this for me. He's wonderful and we are keeping the details of Eve in case it happens another time. Bless John he cuddled me and kissed my tears and fears away, but I'll always remember Naga and what a lovely friendly dog he was.

Soon we will be leaving and I go down to buy a coke and say goodbye to Freda, the girl who has a stand by the beach in front of the hotel. She tells me she is Muslim and lives in Bang Tao but not the strictest sort and only goes to the mosque twice a day and only wears the yashmac at home and in the village.

She tells me we cannot say goodbye as I will be coming back. I hope she is right. I give her a piece of paper with the name of the village and Eve's phone number on it and tell her that if anybody finds Naga and calls Eve we will give them a 2,000 thb reward. We give the same information to the manager at the hotel and he says he will pass on to the security guard as that would entice him to go and look for Naga.

He tells us he hopes the incident did not ruin our holiday and our feelings about the hotel. Apparently he is leaving soon to become GM of a hotel in Phuket Town but promises he will give Eve's number to all the staff. I hope she does not curse us! We will write to her and send her a donation and I'll try and contact the English lady to see if she has a photo of Naga. . .

The runway stretches out in front of us like fairy light. 6:55pm and we're up. 6:58 and the lights of Phuket have gone. Tears and more tears. All I can think of is Naga. I suppose it is not only leaving here but not knowing where or how he is.

These events all took place in March 1998. We wrote to Eve and donated to her fledgling organisation but heard no news of Naga, which, as it turned out, was not surprising.

Six months later and we took a further trip to Phuket in low season. Freda was still there selling drinks and fruit and I went to say hello. The hotel's general manager had gone, as had his Thai deputy. What Freda told me that first day ended any chance of us ever finding Naga again. She had been frightened to tell us what really had happened. Early in the morning, after Naga had come up with us to our room, she had been getting her stall set up and saw a security guard grab Naga and hit him over the head several times then put him in a sack. She had no doubt he was dead.

To say we were shocked is an understatement; it brought home to us just what a desperate life these dogs have. To use a phrase from *Miss Saigon*, they are truly the dust of life in a society that has created them but does not want them.

Naga had been given a few weeks' affection and care in a place that saw him as an unwanted pest.

As soon as the couple who had been looking after him left, his death sentence was sealed. I can believe that the GM just told his Thai assistant to get rid of the dog, and he in turn told his head of security, without maybe realising that get rid of in their eyes meant killing.

Although we were still several years, we thought, from being able to retire here, there is no doubt that Naga was the seed that grew into the flower that is Soi Dog today. As it turned out, it would be less than five years before we were able to move here and start to do something positive for these animals, and by that time the situation was even worse.

# Goodbye Yorkshire, Hello Thailand

The first step of our move to Thailand took place in October 2000. We had got to know a lovely couple called Robert and Busaba, who had opened a restaurant and pub called The Albatross in Canal Village in Phuket, which still exists today, although much changed.

The Albatross became a home from home during our trips to Phuket, and we became great friends with many of the staff there as well.

Robert introduced us to another couple – Andy, a United Airlines pilot, and Napa, his Thai partner, who was a stewardess for the same airline. Both couples had purchased land plots that had been put up for sale by Laguna.

We had already been looking at the local property market, which in those days was still quite small. After visiting their plots and seeing Robert's plans, we were hooked. The land was in a beautiful location overlooking a lagoon and beyond was the Laguna golf course, so unlikely to be spoiled in the future.

Prices in those days were very reasonable and the pound was very strong. Although we thought we were still several years from retirement, it looked like a good investment, and so it proved.

There is no doubt that Laguna regret selling those first plots, as now they are building their own houses and apartments wherever they have land and there are few better spots.

The next step happened in late 2001. John's company was building a new plant in China and downsizing its operations in Europe. They were looking initially for volunteers to accept redundancy. With the package on offer, which included immediate pension without penalty, it was an offer too good to turn down.

John calculated that if he continued to work normally until he was fifty-five and then resign, which was what he originally planned, he would be worse off long term. A bonus was that the company asked him if he would stay on another year to help oversee the changes. That meant a further year's service and pension, and in the meantime we could look to get our house built in Thailand. It was as if everything was meant to happen, and I am sure it was.

The dogs clearly needed us now, not in five or ten years' time.

We had previously met Dieter, a German expat, who had his own construction company in partnership with an old-school Thai builder. By email we designed the house together. Dieter was a typical German: efficient, a stickler for detail, and a hundred percent honest and reliable.

Again, I think it was meant to be. And with what I have learned since with building companies here, we were very lucky.

I wanted a traditional Thai-looking house but with a Western interior. Looking back, we would probably have done things a bit differently having now lived here for almost fifteen years and with the knowledge that we would have a large number of animals living with us.

No doubt what was originally on the plans as John's movie room would have been redesigned as an animal hospital from the beginning, but until you have actually lived in the tropics, it is difficult to understand the impact of the climate or, of course, how your life is going to pan out.

We made two trips to Thailand in 2002 to choose such items such as tiles and paint, bathroom suites, fans, light switches, doors, furniture, and kitchen. In those days it was still necessary to go to Bangkok for some things, but already Western kitchens were on sale in Phuket and what, for me, was the most important room of the house I was able to sort out with a Western company based in Phuket.

In early 2003, having now officially retired, John flew over to oversee the final stages of the build, while I drew the short straw and had charge of selling our house and then packing everything into the boxes, which would fill a twenty-foot container.

I was determined to take everything I could fit in and this included not only large items of furniture, but ornaments, books, videos, kitchen equipment, and Christmas decorations – you name it, I packed it – and I spent weeks carefully filling the boxes.

I bought huge rolls of bubble wrap from a local garden centre and the removals company supplied dozens of cardboard boxes.

If I say so myself, there are few better packers than me, whether it's a suitcase or a container. At the bottom of every box, I packed cans of English beer and bottles of wine, both of which were very expensive in Thailand, and all sorts of food items you couldn't find at that time in Thailand. I would have been very happy with just Thai food but knew John would miss his home comforts.

Selling the house was essential as we had used up all our savings on the house in Thailand and still had a mortgage on our house in England. Although John's pension would cover our day-to-day living in Thailand, we still needed some capital to enable us to start saving dogs.

Fortunately, the house sold quickly to somebody who had no house to sell themselves, so when John returned home in May we were able to pack up the container, which would hopefully arrive shortly after us in Thailand, and make the final arrangements.

Max had passed away two years earlier at the grand old age of fifteen, which is unusual for a Cavalier, but we still had Junkie and Suai and Sanuk and no way were they not coming with us.

During this time, my father had been very supportive and taken a big interest in the house plans and told us to follow our dream. My mother was convinced we had been brainwashed by some weird cult and were moving to live in a remote jungle somewhere. She was against the move from the start.

Despite my mother's best efforts, in early July 2003 the house was empty, container on its way, tickets booked, and, after a farewell party, we were ready.

Saying goodbye to friends, old work colleagues, and relatives is never easy, but it turned out to be a happy occasion even though we didn't know if we would ever see many of them again.

I think they were happy for us and shared our excitement at starting a new life.

When the shipping container arrived it was literally filled to capacity. It was a strange feeling watching our possessions being driven away knowing that the next time we would see them would be in several weeks in a distant land and then re-entering our now virtually empty house.

It is a fact of life in Thailand that everything is always late. It is known as 'Thai time' and the same held true for our house.

We received a message from Dieter a few days before we were about to travel. Could we delay a few weeks?

'No!' was the clear answer. We would make do in a couple of rooms if necessary, but no way could we cancel everything now. Dieter, bless him, found a solution by renting a house for us not far away for a few weeks, so although a bit inconvenient at least we could push ahead.

The plan was that I would go out first with Junkie, and John would drive me to Heathrow Airport and then come out himself two days later with the cats. I have forgotten why we did it that way but there must have been a reason for it.

Spending that last night in a virtually empty house was a strange feeling, not helped by the knowledge that I would be making the journey to Thailand alone.

On our last night in the house, we sat on the floor with our backs against the wall eating a Chinese takeaway and looked back on the happy years we had spent here. To many people a house is just bricks and mortar, but this place was where our life together really started and it held so many precious memories that would remain with us all our lives. What the future held we did not know, but we looked forward with anticipation rather than fear.

We had done all the paperwork correctly for the animals, but I was still a bag of nerves when we checked Junkie in at Heathrow. The Air Canada girl who was checking us in was horrified at the Thai Airways rates, so under-weighed Junkie to bring the cost down, which was still more than my ticket.

The first thing I did on boarding the aircraft was to ask the stewardess to advise the captain there was a dog on board and please to ensure the hold was heated. She did just that and came back to reassure me that the captain was aware and would I like the temperature set at any particular level. When I reached Bangkok, I had to transfer for the onward flight to Phuket and ensured once more that the captain knew he had a precious cargo.

Once in Phuket I fully expected issues, even though all the paperwork was in order, and I was armed with a bundle of 1,000-baht notes just in case. I need not have worried: first the baggage handler, who I had explained to that I had a dog, passed a totally relaxed Junkie in his cage to me, then the customs officer peered in the cage, said how beautiful he was, and waved me through.

As soon as we were outside I let Junkie out of the cage, and bless him it was totally clean but he did have an enormous pee and poop in the car park. I was being picked up by JJ, an English friend who owned a bar in Cherngtalay, and he took me round to the house Dieter had rented for us.

After dropping off the bags, I determined it was time for a drink, so JJ took me and Junkie to his bar. There, an Australian, who I later learned was particularly obnoxious, took one look at Junkie and said, knowingly, 'That dog is not going to survive five minutes in this climate!' I was devastated and panic-stricken. Was he right? I immediately called John in the UK and he told me to ignore him. 'Of course Junkie will be fine.' How right he was.

Junkie loved Thailand and the Thai climate. In England, he would often lie in the garden under a chair if the sun was out. In Thailand, he loved to sunbathe and loved his daily walks on the beach. He also got used to our growing canine family, who all treated him with the respect an older dog deserves. He lived as happy as any dog can be until his heart gave out at the age of thirteen.

John arrived as planned two days later with our cats and again without any issues. Dieter had put up a temporary fence all around the garden of our rented home so we could let the animals out a bit, but I would only let the cats out under close supervision.

On their very first day we watched them scratching at some gravel and then all of a sudden flick a not-small snake into the air. Fortunately, it moved quickly and got through the fence.

John looked it up in a reference book on the snakes of Thailand and it turned out to be one of the most poisonous found here. It was quite amazing how two pedigree cats, born and bred in a country with hardly any snakes and lizards, could revert to natural instincts in dealing with poisonous snakes. When we moved to our own house, the garden was their jungle, and on more than one occasion I saw them literally jumping up and down vertically, almost as if in a dance. The reason? A cobra, which were not unusual and, of course, deadly if they were able to strike first.

It always seemed to happen when John was out, and the worst occasion was when a very large snake came up to the patio. I saw it and immediately grabbed the cats and threw them inside and slammed the door shut. The snake slowly crawled around peering through the windows. It was huge.

John did not believe me and said I was exaggerating, but it was some sort of python and could easily have had both cats for dinner. Somebody told me that when they peer through windows, it means they will come back, but thankfully I never saw it again. This probably gives the impression that we were living in some snake-infested place whereas in reality unless one of the dogs or cats found one, we never saw them and can count encounters each year on one hand.

Suai and Sanuk loved their new home. They were fascinated by the geckos and other small reptiles, of which there were plenty.

The first few weeks in Thailand were focused on seeing the house completed. The container had been stuck in Port Klang in Malaysia but arrived a day after we actually moved in at the end of August, which was perfect timing as it turned out.

The only damage was a small tear to a mattress, which had been placed right at the back of the container, and two bottles of champagne had blown in one of the boxes, no doubt as a result of the heat being stuck on the dock-side in Malaysia. Virtually every box I had put wine and English beer cans in the bottom, as both were expensive in Thailand along with hard-to-get food items. When it comes to packing I have no equal, and what I can get in a suitcase has to be seen to be believed, much to the despair of John, who has to carry them.

During our last stay at the hotel in Phuket, we had mentioned to the staff we knew that we were moving here, and one of the room maids approached us and asked us if we were looking for a part-time maid.

We had already decided that we did not want a full-time, live-in maid, but would like someone to help with the house, so Yao worked for us for four hours every morning before starting work at the hotel.

She had three daughters and was determined that they would not have to work as a cleaner all their lives as she had. Yao's husband was a waste of space and, like many Thai families, it was the woman who supported the family. We have helped her financially over the years, but by largely through her own efforts and hard work, she has seen all her daughters graduate from university with top grades and go on to good careers.

Yao is still with us today and is more a part of the family than a maid. A few years after she started working for us, she finished working for the hotel after completing twenty-five years' service, which gave her a lump sum, and began working for us full-time. She is great with our animals and a lovely lady.

Yao told us we must have the house blessed and any bad spirits removed. Now even I was sceptical about this, but in the corner of the garden we had a traditional Thai spirit house and when in Thailand . . .

A man who was skilled in such matters was called round, and what we expected to be a short ceremony ended up taking nearly all day. Pieces of thread were run around the house, offerings made to the spirits, and firecrackers let off to frighten bad ones away. Every time we thought it must end now, another part of the ceremony began with an awful lot of chanting and prayers. I imagine any evil spirits fled out of boredom. Anyway, our house was blessed, and we still have some paper symbols stuck on one of the house pillars leading upstairs to this day.

As I focused on getting the house as I wanted, John went off to investigate the local dog rescue scene. Eve and Leone were still feeding dogs; Eve at her temples close to where we lived and Leone and her staff all the stray dogs in the south-west, which covered Rawai and Nai Harn.

They were no longer involved in the running of PAWS and advised that it had now become a bit politically complicated. As volunteers, they were allowed to take four dogs per month to the vet for sterilising. Some volunteers did not bother, so Leone would take more and tell the vet to allocate them to another volunteer. It was clear to John that such an arrangement was not going to have any impact on the huge problem that had now developed and decided not to get involved.

He then met a retired English couple who had started an organisation called DIDIT, which stood for Dogs in Distress in Thailand. A bit like Eve, they focused on helping dogs in temples, but by 2003 it was this lovely couple who were in trouble. They had learned the hard way that trying to care for Thai street dogs is exhausting work as well as being financially draining. Sadly, when John met them they had had enough and were making arrangements to move back to the UK.

Before they left, John went out with Eric on one of his feeding runs. He was desperate for somebody to take over feeding dogs at one temple in particular. Wat Para was described on maps as a monks' camping ground and not a temple at all. It was cared for by one monk with occasional visiting monks and he was the only monk on Phuket who did not go out and collect alms.

The reason was that the temple was surrounded by an entirely Muslim village, so people would come from all over to bring food and cleaning materials to him. He was deservedly well respected as a teacher, a true monk, and a lovely man who had many tattoos, which he told us went back to his youth when he was a bad boy.

Every time John went there to feed dogs, he would always come out armed with various food and drink. The monk also cared for the many dogs that lived in the grounds, and Eric was concerned that they would struggle for food if he did not go there.

There had been occasions in the past when locals had poisoned the dogs because they had gone into the village looking for food. If the monk found them in time he would give them leaves from one of the trees, which acted as an emetic, but sadly it often happened at night and he would awake to find one or more dogs dead.

Although, of course, there are many kind Muslims on Phuket, it appears that the imams here must preach that all dogs are unclean and not to be tolerated, as the persecution of dogs is very different to what one sees in other Muslim countries.

In Phuket, woe betide a dog that tries to move into a Muslim area. Of course, this is just another example of religion losing its way. The Koran makes no mention of dogs, and Mohammed preached kindness and tolerance to all living creatures. In one of the *Hadith*, a decree did go out to kill all the dogs in Messina following a rabies outbreak, which was shortly after clarified as being only infected dogs. Why Muslim men don't simply carry out the washing ritual if they come into contact with a dog, I have no idea. Certainly it is contrary to their religion to deliberately kill a dog just for being there. I should add that over the years, we have come across many acts of kindness to dogs by local Muslims, and one of our first vets was Muslim, so this is not universal in Phuket. But it is sadly very common.

John made a commitment to Eric that he would continue to feed the dogs and also took on other temples that he had cared for. John wrote letters to all the hotels in Laguna and made arrangements with the chefs that their staff would put any unwanted meat and leftovers into buckets that he provided. The system worked quite well for many years. The quality and amount varied from hotel to hotel, with the Laguna Beach providing cooked chicken carcasses while the Sheraton would provide raw past-sell-by-date meat, which I would cook up in a large pot that stank the house out.

He even started getting the leftover sandwiches from Thai Airways flights through a friend who worked at the Albatros in the evenings but managed Thai Airways catering in the day.

John would often pick up large bags of these sandwiches, all individually wrapped in cling film, which had to be unwrapped; the cheese and tuna went down well with the dogs, though. Finding supplies of food was always a challenge and required time and effort to do. Today, volunteers are lucky in that we can provide good quality dry dog food, but many Thais still collect leftovers and cook it up as we used to do. There is no doubt that the dogs enjoy it.

Feeding dogs may keep temple dogs from roaming, but it was not the answer to the problem. Puppies were constantly being dumped. John had already started to formulate some ideas and spoken with local vets, when one day in September fate again played a hand.

John was talking to a guy in the pub one evening who mentioned that a woman had been in earlier asking for volunteers to help her carry dogs from nearby Leam Sing beach to her truck. She apparently was taking them to a local vet to have them sterilised. The beach was a well-known spot with backpackers, but required a climb down many steps to get there.

The woman had left her card and John got her number and gave her a call. He arranged to meet her the following afternoon at the pub as he wanted to know more about what she was doing. Helping her get those dogs was no problem, but what were her longer-term plans?

Enter Margot into our lives. The story of how Soi Dog was started is well documented, and although articles appear from time to time calling me and John the founders, this was not the case.

Margot was Dutch by birth but also held an American passport and had, like us, just recently moved to Phuket. Like us too, she and her American husband, who oversaw the Asian operations of one of America's largest corporations, were building their own house, though in their case on a stunning site overlooking both Bang Tao and Surin Bay.

Her husband was still working and rarely there, and Margot was renting a house a few minutes' drive away from us. Prior to moving to Phuket, she had been living in a gated community in Bangkok and had decided she would do something about the local dogs.

For Margot, there was only one solution: CNVR (Capture, Neuter, Vaccinate, Release) – something that John also believed was the only possible solution if carried out in large numbers. Euthanising dogs was contrary to religious beliefs.

Margot got involved with an organisation in Bangkok called Soi Dog Rescue, but not always being the easiest person to get on with, bless her, had fallen out with them and started to work on her own. At her own expense, and with the help and support of her sister and friends in the Netherlands, she would take local dogs to private vet clinics to have them sterilised. In the meantime, her sister registered the organisation in the Netherlands as Stichting Soi Dog, much to the annoyance of Soi Dog Rescue, who changed their name to Soi Cat and Dog Rescue later to make it clearer that they were not the same organisation.

At their first meeting, Margot arrived in her old truck, which had hand-painted pictures of dogs on the side and the words Soi Dog Foundation crudely painted in big letters. She explained her plans and John agreed to help her as opposed to taking over DIDIT which, in reality, would also have meant starting from scratch. It made more sense to work together as they both thought exactly the same way in those days.

Margot was also in discussions with an Australian vet called Alison Montgomery who had started a project on Phuket called the Atigaro Project, named after a famous monk.

Alison had been sterilising dogs in temples by bringing over overseas volunteer vets and nurses to run 'MASH'-type clinics at temples and had managed to sterilise around two thousand dogs in the preceding two years.

She was now moving to Hong Kong for work and had planned to pass on her truck and equipment to PAWS, but she was not happy with the way that they were operating. Having spoken to Margot and seen that she believed in exactly the same thing, Alison decided to pass everything to her, including future enquiries from vets and nurses wanting to volunteer. It was a decision that did not go down well with the PAWS management, and I believe is the reason why they would never cooperate with us.

It was at this point, with our house in order, that I began to get more involved. I had taken a TEFAL course before leaving the UK with an idea that I might teach underprivileged children English while John focused on dogs.

There were, however, already many projects working with orphans and other underprivileged children, and starting a teaching scheme was, I was advised, going to be very difficult and probably not needed.

The thought of helping dogs at clinics really inspired me, and so I was determined to also get involved in this new venture. John purchased another truck, which would be solely for dogs, and I decorated it, tastefully of course, with paw prints and Soi Dog Foundation signs.

In reality, the Soi Dog Foundation did not exist as a foundation in Thailand, and our lawyer was keen to point out that having such a sign on our trucks was illegal. We were never arrested and the signs remained. Two years later, we did become an official Thai foundation.

John and I taught ourselves to blow darts from homemade plastic pipes. Margot was already an accomplished darter. The darts were purchased in the Netherlands and featured syringes into which you would draw up an amount of anaesthetic based on the size of the dog.

The dart is then pressurised using a large syringe as an air pump. The needle has a small hole in the side, over which a silicone seal is placed. You aim to hit the dog on the rump, and as the needle enters, the silicone seal is pushed up and the liquid, under pressure, shoots into the dog.

We practised with old darts filled with water using a sack of rice as a target. Ideally you, or somebody who knows the dog, just picks it up without the need for darting, but feral dogs that you can't get close to we had to dart.

Unless you are lucky and the dart hits a dog's vein, it can take a few minutes, sometimes longer, for the dog to eventually fall asleep, and until it does you have to watch it all the time.

Once the dog is asleep, you simply pick it up, which, with a large dog, is not always easy, and put it in the back of the truck.

When we had no volunteers, we would take dogs to one of two local vets we worked with who were sympathetic and gave us special rates. Increasingly, though, word was spreading, and Alison would also pass on details of vets and nurses wanting to volunteer.

When no nurses were there, we would act as nurses as well as dog-catchers, then shave the dogs and give them the cocktail of drugs we used.

It is quite amazing that ordinary people like us could easily acquire strong opiate-based anaesthetic drugs and pain relief. The local large Thai supermarket called Supercheap sold medical supplies in bulk, including syringes, needles, and scalpels, as well as liquid sterilising fluids for the surgical instruments.

In those days they even sold liquid Valium, which was added to the cocktail of drugs given to the dogs.

Every dog sterilised was tattooed in the ear so that if it was picked up again we would know it had already been done. Fairly obvious in the case of males, but not with females, and it was females we focused on.

Although a more complex operation, they were the ones who were giving birth to puppies, and, to put it bluntly, you only needed one intact male in an area and he would quite happily impregnate every female that came into season.

With their incredible sense of smell, it is said that a dog can detect a bitch on heat from several miles away if the wind is in the right direction. I guess that is exaggerated somewhat, but no doubt they can detect from a significant distance.

I loved these first mobile clinics. We met some wonderful people who gave up their time and holidays to come over and help us. The clinics would be held at schools, temples, or anywhere we could pitch a tent and had access to water.

Sometimes, in the early days, we would use Margot's living room, with the dogs in cages on the veranda. It was at one such clinic that the first of our Thai dogs came to join us.

Ginger and Lucky were puppies dumped at Nai Yang temple where John was also feeding. He brought them to the clinic and we decided because they were so young and were not fully awake, we would keep them overnight before returning them next day. Fatal decision!

I would be a hopeless foster carer. Once they are here they would simply not go back. Nearly all our dogs and cats are ones that needed special attention and nursing at home. In those first three months at the end of 2003, records show we sterilised 134 dogs and forty-one cats. Hardly record-breaking, but a start.

One clinic we had was in Rawai at the council offices where garbage trucks were parked. Leone had organised it and was supplying all the dogs. Wearing her Soi Dog T-shirt proudly, she told us a few days into the clinic that she had been contacted by the chairwoman of another animal charity to advise her she had been expelled for taking dogs to Dr Suchon's clinic in other people's names (as previously mentioned, with their permission, as they weren't taking dogs themselves).

In reality, she had been openly doing this for a long time and she knew very well that the reason for her 'expulsion' was that she had been seen wearing a Soi Dog T-shirt. It was so sad, it was actually funny. Why is that people can't work together for the benefit of a common cause? Is it egotism or what?

I don't know if it is restricted to animal welfare or charities in general, but why can't people who have the same cause work together? I know John tried many times to work with PAWS by suggesting they divide up the island and focus on different areas, but all his efforts came to nothing.

Soi Dog as an organisation is not generally admired for the way it has succeeded and the millions of animals' lives it has improved as a result. More, it is the subject of envy and accusations by people who could never give the same level of commitment needed to make an organisation that successful.

The world is full of well-intentioned people, but good intentions alone never achieved anything.

I am sometimes asked about the best way to start an organisation. My answer is always the same. Don't! Don't unless you are prepared to give everything to it, and even then to ensure it will continue after you have gone, or for sure it will die with you.

I have lost count of the number of organisations just in Thailand that started with the best intentions but then have contacted us asking us to take their animals because they can no longer continue.

Remember: it is about the animals you are helping, not you. There is no room for egotism or self-interest. The greatest examples of animal welfare are people who not only gave everything for their cause, but also ensured it continued after they were gone. This is John's major goal now.

For us, it is all about the animals. The reason I am writing this book is that if you bought it, the profits have gone to help more animals.

In those final three months of 2003 and the whole of 2004, we managed to sterilise 1,312 dogs and cats in Phuket. Hardly numbers that would change Phuket, never mind the world, but I loved those days.

As well as becoming proficient dog-catchers, we also learned how to anaesthetise and give basic treatment. I loved the mobile clinics. They were hard work, but catching a dog on the street and then taking it to the clinic and then taking it back knowing that never again would it produce more and more unwanted puppies gave me a real kick.

When it came to catching dogs, I was the patient one. John would catch the easy ones, but would give up on ones he couldn't catch quickly. I would just sit there and ignore the dog until it forgot I was there and would simply amble past me. Then I would strike and call John and tell him he could come back now and pick up the dog which he had said was impossible to catch. It was great to show him that in some areas I was better than him.

## Our Annus Horribilis

Despite loving what we were doing, 2004 was to become my annus horribilis. It started off badly after I received a call to say my father had been taken into hospital just before Christmas at the end of 2003.

Calls to the hospital and my family indicated that although he was very ill, there was no urgency and I could fly back in the New Year. If anything changed they would let me know in plenty of time. Yet on 26 December 2003, I received a call to say he had died peacefully in his sleep. I was devastated and angry that I had not been able to say goodbye and immediately booked the first available flight back to the UK. I knew that neither my mother nor sister would be able to cope with organising the funeral and all those other legalities that have to be taken care of after a death.

England was suffering a severe cold snap, and arriving from hot and dry Thailand felt like arriving on another planet. I had already determined I could not spend even two or three weeks with my mother, but happily some very good friends who lived a few minutes' drive away from her put me up.

David and Pauline turned up the central heating and left it on twenty-four hours a day, despite melting themselves. They also loaned me a car so I could visit my mother and take care of all the arrangements.

I loved my dad very much and losing him was a big blow. I had often wished that he'd met somebody else as he certainly did not deserve my mother. With Dad gone, her only concern seemed to be who was going to take her to the shops as she couldn't drive.

It was obvious she felt that I should move back to England to take care of her, which was definitely not going to happen.

After organising Dad's funeral and taking care of all the legal issues, I was going back home to Thailand just as soon as I could. Selfish? Maybe, but my mother was fit and healthy and lived on a bus route, which is how she usually went shopping, and my sister and other relatives also lived nearby.

I flew back to Thailand the middle of January and I wouldn't return to England again for another eleven years. With the death of my father, any motivation to go back had gone.

The UK had nothing for me now – Thailand was my home and I knew I had a purpose in life.

I have never regretted moving here; in fact, many Thai friends believe I must have been Thai in a previous life, and from the day we arrived, it felt like I was coming home.

Yes, there are issues in dealing with the language, and the officialdom can drive you to despair at times, but I love this country and nothing would persuade me to leave.

John would continue to return each year to see his mother and sons, while his sister would come over most years to visit us, but that was it

Returning home to Thailand, I immediately threw myself back into running the mobile clinics. My bossy personality meant I quickly organised what tasks John, me, and Margot would do, which also depended on what additional help we had. Sometimes we would have vet nurses as well as vets, and at the south of the island Leone and her staff ensured a plentiful supply of dogs and cats. Darting was my favourite task, but this was also to nearly cost me my life.

Our 'family' was also increasing in size. Firstly, John found a tiny black puppy lying in the gutter outside Ban Don Temple where it had presumably been dumped. It had been hit by a car and both back legs were broken.

John took it to Dr Trethep's surgery and christened it Nid Noi ('Little Bit' in Thai). We would go and visit each day and take him some barbecue chicken. After a few weeks when he was able to walk again we couldn't very well put him back where we found him, could we?

Nid Noi he may have been at that time, but he was to grow into a strapping alpha male who would not have looked out of place in a dog-fighting ring.

Not long after that, when John was feeding at Nai Yang temple one day, a monk came out holding a small black dog that John knew lived on the garbage tip behind the temple. One of her back legs was covered in blood, the foot badly mangled. It was thought she had caught it in a motorcycle wheel. John took her to the vet and again we would visit regularly. Dam Dam ('Black Black' in Thai) knew how to get sympathy and still does to this day. After a few days, the vet advised that she could be released, but not back onto a rubbish tip until the wounds had fully healed, which could be weeks. Could we maybe treat her at home until fully healed? You know the rest. To this day, Dam Dam, when looking for sympathy, will carry her back leg and look mournfully at you. How could we possibly take a little dog that could only use three legs and put her back on the rubbish tip? We can't, John, can we?

So we now had five dogs and two cats. Two cats, sadly, were soon to become one.

One day, Suai, the older of the two cats I had brought from the UK, simply disappeared.

I spent hours walking the streets calling for him. We put reward posters up everywhere offering the equivalent of a month's salary for a local Thai if they found him.

However, all that achieved was that someone saw Sanuk outside our gate and, assuming it was Suai, picked him up and took home with the intention of claiming the reward. Fortunately, Yao, our maid, heard about it and got him back before we even knew he had gone.

I also received an email from one sick individual telling me sorry but he and his Thai boyfriend had seen him and decided to eat him for dinner. He told me he tasted delicious.

Being as gullible as I can be at times, I believed it, until John convinced me that it was just some sick person deliberately trying to upset me. Well, he certainly succeeded. John tried to trace where the message had originated from, but the internet provider was not prepared to tell.

As I'm sure any pet owner will tell you, it is the not knowing what happened that is the worst, and we never did see Suai again.

Had he had one fight too many with a snake? Had a python caught him? Had somebody passing by taken a fancy to him and taken him home? If so, was he being looked after properly and did the owners realise he had been castrated so could not be bred from? Would he have a happy life or be kept in a cage?

Questions like this spun through my mind and sadly were never answered. Sanuk died a few years later. He was well used to walking up and down the quiet street outside our house. Our dogs did not bother him, and he would have made short work of the shih-tzu next door. Further down were two large black Labradors, but they were always locked in the garden, only one day the maid forgot to lock the gate and they saw Sanuk and attacked him.

Our maid, Yao, came in the house in hysterics. I grabbed Sanuk and John drove like a maniac to our vet but it was too late. Sanuk had gone. Should I have even brought them to Thailand? Should I have made sure they were kept securely locked in the house? People do keep just house cats, but they both loved to go out and also visit our neighbours; keeping them locked inside would have been torture for them. Again, I was devastated. But they were used to going out and they would have hated being locked up. Not knowing what happened to Suai will always haunt me, but they had wonderful lives – if shorter than they should have been – and I just have to accept that. It still hurts, though, and I often find myself thinking about them, particularly wondering if Suai is still alive somewhere.

Back to 1993. They say everything comes in threes. Well, I had lost my dad and then Suai, surely nothing else could happen that year. How wrong can you be? Religious people will say that bad things are sent by God to test us. I don't believe that, but if it were true then boy was God out to test me.

Thanks to Alison we were receiving a steady stream of volunteer vets. Towards the end of September, we had three experienced vets coming over along with three vet nurses. We were going to be busy.

We arranged to use a school hall at Ban Don School as the clinic site. Eve and Rock would provide lunches and drinks and Margot, John, and I would go out and catch the dogs. I was to be assisted by an occasional volunteer who I shall call Pete (not his real name) as I had fallen a few days earlier and my ribs were very sore. Pete used to like to volunteer, occasionally darting dogs.

An American expat who spoke fluent Thai, he earned the nickname GI Pete as he always arrived with a bandana tied around his head and a military-style belt that gave him the appearance of a character out of Rambo.

On this day he was wearing sparkling white trainers with matching shorts and T-shirt.

'Not exactly darting clothes, Pete,' I remarked.

'Don't worry, Gill, I'll just dart the dogs and you can pick them up,' he replied.

Having already carried out a reconnaissance, I was aware of a large female dog that had obviously had litters of pups previously hanging out in a builder's yard. I had tried but failed to catch her once before. This time I was determined. Pulling up outside the yard, I told Pete to stay there while I quietly crept around looking for her. I found her asleep in one of a pile of large concrete drainpipes that were for sale. It was an easy shot. Oblivious to my presence, her rump made an easy target.

Now, when you dart a dog, one of two things happen. Either you are very lucky and the anaesthetic goes immediately into an artery or blood vessel and the dog goes down in seconds, or, more often, and as in this case, the anaesthetic goes into the muscle and it can take minutes, even longer, before the dog eventually falls asleep.

Now, when you have suddenly had somebody shoot a needle into your rump, you don't simply relax and chill out and wait for sleep to take over. If you are a dog, you get the hell out of there as fast as you can.

For the darter, it is important not to chase after the dog but just to keep it in your sights. If you chase it, it will run faster and there's a good chance that the adrenalin will mean it never actually goes to sleep.

The problem here was that this was the end of September, which is at the height of the rainy season, and next to the builder's yard was one of the myriad of former rice paddies that can be found throughout the rural areas of Phuket.

Today they are either being filled in for building or are used for grazing water buffaloes, which are never happier than wallowing in muddy fields.

Sod's law that this dog took off into the flooded water buffalo field. I watched her run off for around a hundred metres and then begin the tell-tale drunken stagger indicating she would soon collapse. I shouted to Pete, 'You need to go get her before she collapses!'

'Go in there? You must be joking,' he said, pointing at his sparkly trainers.

I sighed. There was only one thing for it: I would have to go and get her or she would drown for sure. She was still splashing around when I reached her so I waited until she began to sink and quickly grabbed her under the front legs and began to drag her towards the road. The pain in my ribs was not pleasant, to put it mildly, and neither were Pete's encouraging calls of 'Atta girl, Gill, not far to go now'.

I got her into the back of the truck and we drove her immediately to the clinic site, which was only two minutes away. I looked a real sight. My trousers from the knee down were covered in mud and my shoes were full of it. I took great pleasure in getting a handful of mud and throwing it on to Pete's still-pristine white T-shirt. He may not have been amused but everybody else was, and he was ribbed incessantly for playing the tough GI character but leaving me to get the dog.

Other than the dog being sterilised and putting her back in the builder's yard to never have puppies again, that should have been the end of it. But it was only the beginning.

Two days later, the very successful clinic ended with a record number of dogs sterilised. I mentioned to John that I was feeling a bit off, almost as if I was starting with flu. However, in two days' time it was John's birthday, and I was determined that we would combine it with a belated house-warming with more than a hundred guests invited.

The next best thing for me to catching dogs was preparing food for a large party, and so I was working around the clock for two days to get everything prepared.

On the evening of John's birthday everything was ready except me. I felt awful and told John I would have to go to bed. Missing a party is not something I do lightly but I felt really ill. I told him I was sure it was just flu and I would take the usual meds and not to worry about it. The party was a roaring success but I missed out on it.

The following day, I felt no better, and John started to insist I go to the hospital and get properly checked out. Initially I refused, but early evening the pain in my legs became excruciating and I told John to get me down there. We stopped off and picked up Khun Yud, a good friend and the partner of JJ, landlord of the local pub. She sat with me in the back while John drove to the hospital. I was taken into casualty, where we literally watched my arms and legs change from a normal flesh colour to a shade of grey. That was about the last thing I remembered for over four weeks. I was put into an induced coma and taken straight to ICU.

So what had actually happened? You see local people wading through fields all the time, often fishing, as although these fields are bone-dry throughout the dry season, once flooded, fish appear as if by magic.

I had been infected by an unidentified soil- or water-based gram-negative bacteria, which can apparently enter the body through the pores of your skin. I was a bit rundown at the time with a cracked rib and my immune system, which was not great at the best of times, was already compromised. Had Pete or somebody else gone in to get the dog, then other than getting dirty, chances are they would have fought off the bacteria naturally and been unaware of it.

In my case, however, the bacteria multiplied, attacking my vital organs, and my immune system could not cope with it. I was told that part of the body's defence system is to send blood from non-vital organs such as arms and legs to try to save the ones that are vital to life. A condition known as septic shock kicks in, which also causes the blood-clotting system to go into overdrive, blocking the myriad small veins in the limbs.

With the bacteria being unidentified, doctors were also struggling to find the right antibiotic, and over the next weeks had extremely powerful medication flown in from Australia. Apparently starting me on antibiotics before taking blood samples also made it harder to identify.

If I was in septic shock, then John was in emotional shock. One minute I had been complaining of flu-like symptoms, the next I was in intensive care on a life-support system.

The doctor in charge advised John that I was in a critical condition and that my chances of survival were around one in ten. Even if I did survive then it was likely I would lose both my arms and legs. Some choice, eh?

One very positive thing was that in times like this the expat community certainly pull together, and although at hospital twenty-four hours a day, John was never alone.

On day three, with my heart already having stopped on more than one occasion, John received a call from James Batt, the CEO of Laguna and also a member of the hospital board. He advised John that although the hospital was an excellent provincial one, he strongly suggested that I look to get me evacuated to Singapore. Having been told the previous night that there was no doctor on duty, and the one in charge of my case had gone to a different province where he also had patients, John contacted our medical insurance company, which agreed, and suggested that they get me to Bumrumgrad Hospital in Bangkok.

John consulted James, who said that would be a good choice.

The local hospital was not happy with the decision and said it was too dangerous to move me, but as John pointed out, having been told I had little chance of survival, and Bumrumgrad having its own air ambulance with specialist team, that is what was going to happen.

Sadly, with these international hospitals it often seems to be more about profit, and no doubt they were losing what would be a good source of revenue if I survived.

It was to be my first and only time in a private jet but I knew nothing about it, not even a glass of champagne. The team from Bumrumgrad arrived under the command of a former Thai Air Force doctor whose expertise was to evacuate patients this way. Every piece of equipment had to be switched over to smaller versions, and once that was all done, the police were contacted to confirm that the road to the airport was clear as it had been a stormy evening in Phuket.

The plane was a flying intensive care unit. I was on a bed in the middle surrounded by the team, who were constantly monitoring all the different machines keeping me alive at that point.

I am not sure if all hospitals are the same, but in Bumrumgrad I had a general practitioner overseeing my case who pulled in all the different specialists that were needed. He would chair the meetings, and John told me later that he had never seen so many different doctors in one night. At Bumrumgrad it was very different to the hospital in Phuket, but even so, John was told to expect the worst.

I, of course, knew nothing about what was happening. John was at my bedside most of the time, going off only to grab a few hours' sleep in a nearby guest house. His sister, herself an intensive care nurse, flew over to support him and also explained what the hospital was doing. Occasionally, I would become delirious and they had to tie my arms to the bed to ensure I did not try to pull any tubes out, which I apparently fought against. I have vague memories of nightmares of being unable to move and also seeing giant spiders on the cupboard at the end of the bed, but not much else.

Early November and I started to come round. Although I was still heavily sedated, the incubator was removed and I could recognise visitors. I had clearly not died and the worst things at that point were a huge bedsore on my lower back and that my thick, long hair was completely matted. Nobody had thought to keep it groomed and most of it had to be cut off, which did nothing to help my demeanour.

I was aware that my arms and legs were heavily bandaged and although my arms looked a mess, it was clear I was not going to lose them. They would remain heavily scarred where the patches of gangrene had been, but I was able to move my hands OK.

However, my legs were a different matter. I could see when they changed the dressings that they were totally black up to my knees, and a few days after regaining consciousness I was advised by the surgeon that at least one would need to come off, though hopefully below the knee. The other he would investigate during surgery, but it was possible he might just need to remove part of the foot. The surgery would wait until I was well enough and could be moved to a general ward.

If the nursing care in ICU was great (excepting my hair), in the general ward it was non-existent. Most Thais have family members who come in to give twenty-four-hour care. John could not do that so he hired a private nurse to stay with me at night. Come the day of surgery and, of course, I was frightened. I was desperate to keep at least one leg, and on waking up the first thing I asked was: 'Had he saved it?' John shook his head, and for the first time I cried. John was a typical man, and instead of giving me the sympathy I wanted, told me to pull myself together and get over it or words to that effect. I hadn't died and life would go on.

To say I was angry is an understatement. John is probably more sensitive than most men, but he had simply no understanding at all that I was grieving and needed his support, not his stupid practical statements.

He could apologise all he wanted but I would never forgive him for that. All I had wanted was a cuddle and his reassurances that he still loved me. When it comes to the beauty stakes I am no great shakes, but if I had one strong point it was my legs and now they had gone. Maybe I had been lucky, and yes I would fight back, but at that moment all I felt was loss.

Other than waiting for the wounds to heal, that should have been it, but never one to do things by halves, I developed severe pneumonia and had to be put back in ICU on a ventilator again.

Again, John was told it was extremely serious and I was in a critical condition. Well, I had not come that far to throw in the towel, and gradually my lungs began to clear. In two weeks I was back on a general ward. John had bought a wheelchair and was able to take me to the hospital's gardens, which were on a balcony.

Being me and having now recovered from pneumonia, I wanted a cigarette. It was now a question of waiting for wounds to heal. I was also introduced to a lovely Thai prosthetist who worked for the German prosthetics company Otto Bock, which had a facility in Bangkok.

He advised me that it would be several weeks before they could actually make legs for me as they needed the stumps to fully heal and, in effect, shrink in size. To help, I was given elasticated bandages and had to wrap them tightly to form a cone shape.

He also told me that it would not be easy learning to walk again with two prosthetics, which is far harder than learning to use one, and that a large percentage of people gave up and just used a wheelchair. He said to me, 'But I don't think you will be doing that,' and I assured him that I would not.

One advantage was that I could choose my height. I had always been tall and he said a lower centre of gravity could help so we decided I would lose two inches.

Early in December, a bizarre situation occurred, and for three days I was to have a roommate: John! He had gone back to his room one evening and grabbed something to eat. The following morning he felt extremely ill and had got severe food poisoning. The doctor at the hospital wanted to admit him, and when they found out that I was a patient as well, they moved him into my room so we could keep each other company.

We must have looked a strange sight heading for the gardens, with John pushing my wheelchair with one hand and his IV fluid stand with the other.

I was becoming desperate to go home. It was now more than two months since I had seen my 'babies' and I wanted to get on with my life, whatever that might be. I told my main doctor that I was definitely going home for Christmas. I had invited our single friends around for Christmas dinner and nothing was going to stop me.

He said, 'We will see.' In the meantime, John organised what he christened 'the Great Escape'. Patients were not allowed outside the hospital grounds, but I was determined to go have a drink at the bar John used next to where he was staying, just around the corner from the hospital. He had done a recce and worked out how to do it. He had got some clothes for me so helped me to get dressed, and then after checking the coast was clear, pushed me out as though going to the garden, but on entering the lift instead pressed for the floor that linked to the multi-storey car park and one or two outpatient clinics.

Having got that far it was into another lift then out on to the street, and then round the corner and we were there. The owner of the bar and the staff were expecting me and it became a regular nightly event for the rest of my stay.

On 20 December, I told the doctor that I was leaving next day and asked John to book flights. After a lot of discussion, the doctor could see that my mind was made up and, although against his wishes, agreed I could leave on 22 December to allow him time to sort out all the medical supplies and tablets and also for the hospital to arrange flights and ambulance to the airport. I would need a wheelchair to my seat, but no private jet this time. Time enough for me to sort out Christmas as well.

My main doctor was a Sikh, who had been educated about Soi Dog and seen all the photos of the dogs. He said, 'I don't know what you believe in, if anything, but all the doctors here thought you would not survive when you arrived. I believe God has a purpose for you that has not yet been fulfilled, and I think we both know what that is.' I told him he was right. I did have a purpose and I would fulfil it.

Over the years that followed, I was asked many times that if I knew then what I know now would I have still gone in that flooded field? I honestly don't think twice about the answer. Of course, had I known what was going to happen I would have worn a wet suit to prevent any infection, but I didn't. I had darted that dog and no way could I leave her to drown. If the same situation occurred today then I would do the same thing again, but with the advantage that no way can bacteria go through metal legs.

On 22 December, I arrived home in a wheelchair. I would have to go back to get my legs fitted and start learning to walk again towards the end of January.

The welcome from the dogs and cats was amazing. John was dispatched to the shops and I began to prepare for Christmas Day. Yao, bless her, had got decorations down and decorated the house and the tree. Luckily, as always, I had bought presents months before. Cooking and decorating the table from a wheelchair was not easy, but by kneeling on the seat, which is probably not the safest thing to do in a wheelchair, I got by, and everybody seemed to enjoy their dinner as much as I did making it for them. I do love catering for lots of people and get a real kick out of seeing everyone enjoy it.

It had been a great Christmas and I went to bed tired but happy that night, little knowing what the next day would bring.

Boxing Day is a very UK holiday. Nothing to do with pugilism, but named after boxes, as traditionally people would give Christmas gifts (boxes) on Boxing Day.

We were going to lunch at JJ's bar as it was traditional for JJ to put on a spread for his regular customers.

We had a lie in and were having coffee on the balcony. In front of us we could see golfers and their caddies walking along the golf course and everything looked normal. John's telephone rang. It was Yao, who was having a day off. She asked if we were OK, and when we asked why, she said there had been a big wave and some people had been killed.

I told her it had clearly not affected Laguna as people were playing golf and we could see gardeners in the distance tidying up the grounds. Everything looked normal.

We thought no more about it other than on the way to JJ's we decided to drive down to the beach near Laguna where there were many local restaurants.

True enough, obviously there had been a high wave as staff were cleaning up and you could see some broken tables and chairs, but nothing serious.

It was the same when we arrived at JJ's. People had heard there had been an abnormal wave, but nobody thought it was anything to worry about. Life continued as normal for a few hours anyway.

Late afternoon, John got a call from Margot. Leone had been killed going to help tourists and cleaning up on the beach after the first wave. Also Brian, a volunteer vet from London, had been rescued by Rock from the roof of his chalet in Bang Tao only a couple of miles down the road.

I was devastated to hear of Leone's death; we had been talking every day by phone since I had come out of ICU. Her husband, who worked on an oil rig, had previously suffered a stroke and was also recently back home after being first airlifted to Singapore.

We had actually joked that Leone and John could go out and catch dogs while her husband and I underwent our physio sessions. John also called Rock and told him to bring Brian to our house. The party was very much over. We went home and turned on the TV to see what the abnormal wave was and discovered that in fact a full-blown tsunami had caused massive destruction, and, as everybody now knows, became the deadliest in history killing more than 230,000 people.

On that first day details were sketchy and I was in shock over Leone. Brian arrived and described how he had seen the wave coming in and managed to climb onto the roof of his bungalow, which was set back from the sea. Most of the bungalows were severely damaged. It appeared that the ferocity of the wave and the damage caused varied considerably on Phuket. Most of Kamala on the beach side was destroyed, including the large school which, fortunately being a Sunday, was closed.

In Laguna, the Dusit Hotel, including 'our room', which was only yards from the beach, had some broken glass and flooding but no serious injuries. In relation to the number of people on the island, the death toll on Phuket was relatively low.

We spoke to Margot, who was in touch with the feeders we knew, and it appeared that most of the dogs on Phuket had survived and, along with other animals, had fled before the wave hit.

There are many stories regarding animals during the tsunami. The dogs at Kamala temple, which is next to the school and also close to the beach, apparently climbed up the bell tower. Some monks at the temple were killed but not one dog.

A baby elephant at the Dusit Hotel picked up a young girl and carried her away from the sea. People spoke of seeing snakes heading for higher ground. Do animals have a sixth sense that we have lost?

With restaurants washed away and tourists gone, the dogs that lived on the beaches had lost their food source. Margot started organising food relief, while John went online appealing for vets and aid.

The next day, news began to come in that the resort of Kao Lak, around eighty kilometres from Phuket and stretching for around twelve kilometres along the coast, was virtually destroyed and the death toll was massive.

John and I joined some others and drove up there to help. There was not a lot I could do in a wheelchair, but John dropped me off at the local hospital, which looked more like a war zone.

I am not a trained counsellor but did understand trauma and was able to talk to people who had lost limbs and provide a shoulder to those who were desperately searching for family and friends. (The 2012 film *The Impossible* accurately portrays the conditions at the hospital at that time.)

John and the others went to help in the wrapping of the hundreds of bodies, stacked up on a piece of land on the other side of the road to where the Royal Thai Navy boat that was washed ashore stands to this day. Hundreds of photos of missing friends and relatives were posted on a large makeshift notice board.

It was a case of cutting up sheets of muslin and plastic, picking a body up and laying them on it, then wrapping the body and tying it up with string. A local rescue worker would cut off some hair and tie it in a numbered small bag, which was tied to the body, and the volunteers then carried the bag to another row, and so it went on.

The sweet, sickly smell of death was everywhere and helpers were advised to rub Tiger Balm under their nostrils. As you picked a body up, the skin would often slip off. Although the bodies were decomposing, you could still tell foreigners from Thais.

Death draws no distinction. Most heartbreaking were the tiny children, of which there were many. As rescuers worked, more trucks came in bringing more bodies. People were searching the fields behind the now destroyed resorts.

One day, John and a few others went to help another friend who had brought up huge pumps from the golf course where he worked.

The newly opened Sofitel Hotel, famed for having the largest swimming pool in Asia, had been all but destroyed, and they needed to pump out water from under the rooms where it was feared many bodies had been washed into.

A poor Russian lady, who had just arrived, was searching for signs of her son, his wife, and their children. The bedroom interiors were all destroyed and personal belongings, including Christmas wrapping, were strewn everywhere. More than two hundred people died in that hotel alone. Other hotels had been literally wiped off the face of the earth.

As often occurred there during those days, people began to scream that another wave was coming and set off a panic. Many local people refused to come down from the hills for weeks.

We were contacted by the editor of the local newspaper who wanted to know what was needed. John told him proper body bags would speed up the operation.

On the fourth day the first rescue teams began to arrive from overseas armed with body bags, and John decided that we had done all we could do there for now. It was time to go back to helping the dogs.

Offers of help were coming in and vets and nurses arriving. Going to have my legs fitted would have to be postponed. John flew to Bangkok armed with two empty suitcases and was able to fill them with drugs for the dogs.

In those days it was easy for anybody to buy restricted anaesthetic drugs over the counter at pharmacies or have them delivered to your hotel room. We worked almost around the clock; I was managing one clinic while Margot managed another.

At night we would catch up on correspondence and thank people who were offering to help, either by providing time or donating money. Previously, the only fundraising had been organised by Margot's sister in the Netherlands and was tiny. All of a sudden people were offering us donations as they looked for organisations that were helping on the ground.

Phuket as a province is totally dependent on tourism. It had grown rich on tin in the nineteenth century, but the tin had long gone and rubber had replaced it as the main industry.

With the coming of the tourist boom, thousands of workers were needed and they poured down from other regions to fill the gap. The tsunami hit right at the start of the high season, which, of course, was over for that year at least. With no work there was now a mass exodus of Thais who returned to their home provinces.

Some of these Thais owned or at least fed dogs. The dogs were left behind so, rather than treatment, the big need was for food and to sterilise as many dogs as possible while we had so many vets coming to help.

We had three clinics running simultaneously at times, both on Phuket and off it. A wealthy friend, who had been involved in the relief effort at Kao Lak, owned a large motor cruiser, and we had heard that the famous Phi Phi islands had also been decimated with large loss of life.

It was years since we had visited these islands on our first trip to Thailand, and since then the main island had boomed with a small town and many hotels and guesthouses built. The local people were mainly Muslim so there were very few dogs on the island, but we knew there were many cats.

With most people having been evacuated, the concern was for food for the animals. John and a small team of volunteers, including Marc Abraham, who some years later was to find fame as a TV vet in the UK, set off with the boat loaded with food.

There were some local people still on the island feeding the cats so we passed all the food on to them. An abandoned small kitten that had obviously lost its mother and needed milk was taken back with us. The small town was wrecked. Apparently, waves had swept across the island from both directions. Divers who were unaware of what was going on above them surfaced to find their boats gone and bodies floating in the water.

On this one small island, it is estimated more than two thousand people died on that day with over 1,200 people still missing six months later. The true death toll in Thailand will never be known, and nowhere was the reason for this more obvious than in the fishing villages along the coast north of Kao Lak.

When we had last been to Kao Lak in the first days after the tsunami had struck, the temples along the road were burning bodies twenty-four hours a day, and it is believed many were never identified. The fishing villagers had thousands of migrant, often illegal, workers mainly from Myanmar, for whom there were no records.

We had set up a mobile clinic in a temple on the edge of Ban Nam Khem, one of the larger fishing villages, a few weeks after the tsunami. The actual village had virtually disappeared and there were many large trawlers hundreds of feet inland. Local people who had survived were living in makeshift camps, and we came across more than one person who made a daily trip back to the site of their former home to take food for their dog as they were not allowed to keep them in the camp.

In the temple grounds, people were coming to dig up bodies that they had temporarily buried so they did not rot in the heat before they could have a proper funeral and cremation at the temple.

All along the roads, piles of coffins were everywhere along with fleets of refrigerated trucks. Police and forensic scientists had been drafted in from all over the world to start the process of trying to identify the dead and reunite the remains with their families, a process that was to last for many years. If the tsunami brought forward many tales of bravery and heroism, its aftermath was to leave a bad taste in the mouth as corruption took hold.

Ten years later, when meeting with the secretary to the new prime minister, John met a former resident of Ban Nam Khem in the waiting room, still trying to get her promised compensation.

With the fishermen gone it did not take long for the land-grabbers to step in and claim the land for developing into new hotels. Nobody will ever know how many billions of dollars were donated to help the victims of the tsunami. What is known is that very little found its way to those that needed it most, and many government officials became very rich around the region.

Small local charities did their best, some friends of ours building new boats for those fishermen that had lost their livelihoods. Even in the animal welfare field the large charities had a field day, raising record amounts in donations but failing to spend it on where it was intended.

One large charity, then known as the World Society for the Protection of Animals (WSPA) did at least send representatives over, who admitted that they had raised a huge amount of money to the detriment of other funds and that they had to invest at least some of it in the region. Although they had no programmes themselves, they worked by giving grants to member societies and were therefore looking for local charities who would become members so they could give them some funds.

The money, I was told, was literally burning a hole in their pocket as some of the funds were restricted in how they could be used. So it was that out of something bad something good can occur, as although, looking back, the two-year tsunami recovery grant we received was not that large, we were able to employ two full-time vets and two dog-catchers. This would see the number of animals we could sterilise drastically increase.

We had also found a large former detached restaurant in Phuket City with a bit of land at the side. It was like a large empty barn inside, and we decided to rent it as not only a clinic but also as somewhere for the growing number of abandoned dogs to stay, at least temporarily.

Of course, when people heard what was happening more dogs appeared, often thrown over the fence at night, which resulted in one dog being found dead next morning with a broken back. It was clear this could not go on forever. As a temporary holding facility it was OK, but as a shelter it was not, and there was no way Margot wanted a shelter.

I disagreed as it had long been something Leone and I had dreamed of: a sanctuary for abandoned puppies that were so numerous in those days. Don't get me wrong, I understood Margot's point of view – spending money on a shelter meant less being spent on sterilising more dogs and solving the underlying problem. But what were we going to do with the dogs that could not survive on the street? And what were we going to do with the dogs in our care now, most of which we had no idea where they had originally come from? The temples certainly did not want more dogs, and there was no way we could simply just dump them randomly in a place they did not know.

Just Gill

First photo with adoptive
parents 1959

First day at work at
Barclay's Bank 1974

Gill's first Cat and soulmate, Crystal

Gill with her natural brother, Kim, who John traced down
1993

Very early days at John's cottage 1992

Our favourite walk at the top of Ingleborough 1995

Where it all started
The Punch Bowl,
York

Gill's diary entry writing
about helping dogs in
Phuket before moving

On Top of the world.
Lake District 2000

Arriving home after losing legs 2004

Christmas with the Dalley family in Phuket

Gill with dogs at the Government Dog Pound in 2006.

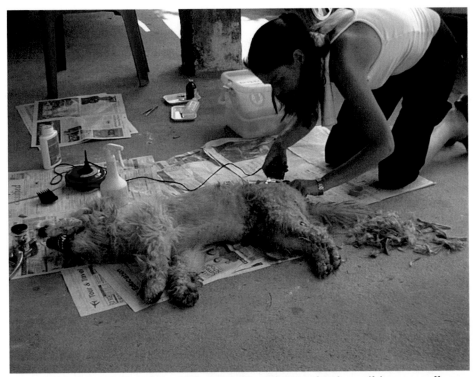

An early mobile clinic. Gill never let a dog go back until it was well groomed as well as neutered. 2004

Managing a mobile clinic after the tsunami 2005

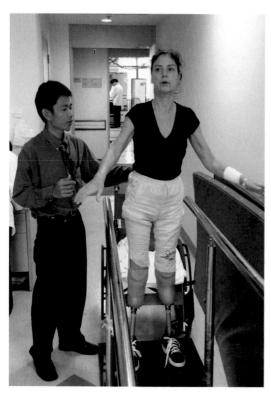

No hands; feels very strange! 2004

Ginger who never left her side
when she lost her legs

Teaching Children at every opportunity 2005

Soi Dog's classroom at the dog pound 2006

Meeting fellow double amputee, Cola, in Bangkok 2016

Rescuing a dog during Bangkok floods 2011

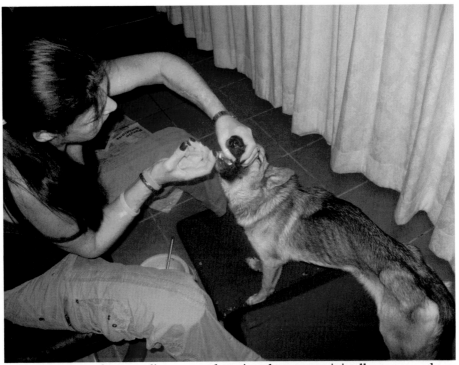

Treating one of many distemper dogs in what was originally supposed to be John's home cinema. Gill had other ideas!

Being awarded First Asia Pacific Hero award Chengdu China 2011

Entrance sign at SDF in Phuket

Laying the cornerstone of new vet hospital 2014

Gill's state of the art veterinary hospital opens at SDF Phuket 2016

In one of the dog runs in Phuket 2016

Gill with Cola on the beach 2016

Gill with Polo when she
arrived at shelter.

Love at first sight. Donna meets Polo at John and Gill's home.

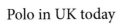

Polo in UK today

Reunited with Milo at SDF Reunion in Wakefield June 2014

Gill and Donna, Ross-on-Wye 2015

Gill at Ross-on-Wye
Funday/Reunion 2015

John views the original
clay model at Albano Poli's
studio; Verona, Italy 2017

Ross-on-Wye 2016. A favourite picture of John's

John's personal tribute to Gill, unveiled on what would have been her
59th birthday. January 29th 2018

Gill's last note and instructions
2017

The final note left for John
scribbled on her latest plan

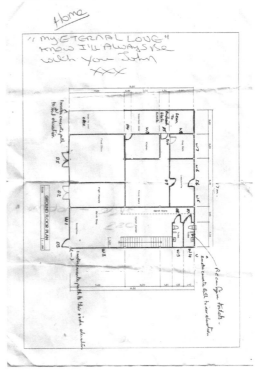

Traffic was stopped for her final journey 2017

Gill's funeral; John's final goodbye

Favourite place...with the dogs

An expression everyone knows!

# Setting up Soi Dog shelters

With the immediate rush of vets and other volunteers, I was able to turn my attention back to learning to walk. Managing mobile clinics in my chair or on my knees was not what I wanted to be doing.

We had cancelled the original hospital appointment back in Bangkok as we were too busy, but at the end of March, John made an appointment and we returned to the capital to meet up with my Thai prosthetist and have my legs made.

He warned me that learning to walk with two false legs was around three times as hard as learning to walk with one, and most of his patients gave up and stuck to using a wheelchair.

'Somehow,' he said, 'I don't think you are going to be one of them.'

I assured him in no uncertain terms that I was not. Even just standing holding on to parallel bars felt very strange as well as uncomfortable. I was determined, though, and after a few days was able to progress to walking with the aid of tripod walking sticks.

Various small modifications were made to the sockets, and after a week I was told I could go home and continue practising there, though I would have to make regular trips back to have the legs checked and the sockets adjusted. It really was like learning to walk all over again.

Back home I would walk up and down the road with the aid of the tripod sticks until I felt confident enough to try without, holding on to John's shoulders.

I hadn't bargained on how hot my stumps would get encased in a flexible silicone liner and then covered in a woollen one to ensure a tight fit.

The heat led to sweat, which led to sores and blisters, and my stumps were soon covered in plasters.

I was determined not to stop, though. I was not going to be confined to a wheelchair all my life, and I was not returning to the UK, where the climate might be kinder on my stumps but not on the rest of me.

I was determined to prove my doctor wrong. Far from putting my legs on the shelf, I wanted to put my wheelchair in the attic not to be seen again.

By September that is what happened and I never saw that wheelchair again until 2017, when I was too ill to use my legs.

A problem I did have, which is apparently very common and that people find hard to understand, was phantom pains. These happened mainly at night and felt like electric shocks in my feet, which, of course, were no longer there.

They were extremely painful and somebody recommended acupuncture as a cure. I had never had acupuncture but was willing to give it a try. The sessions lasted over an hour and the acupuncturist warned I would feel very tired afterwards. He was right, but I have to say it worked. The principle is that when a leg is amputated the brain still thinks it is there, and the body's natural energy flow has been severed. The purpose of acupuncture is to reconnect this energy flow. Now you can believe this or not, but phantom pains are very real and very common, and after a few sessions mine stopped and never happened again.

Back at Soi Dog our new teams were working well. Through contacts and a local lawyer, Margot established Soi Dog as an official Thai foundation with a Thai board, plus herself and John.

Things were not going well for Margot personally, however. The effects of working around the clock for the past year, as well as looking after her own thirteen dogs and overseeing the construction of her house, were taking their toll.

On top of all this, her marriage broke up. It was not surprising that she wanted to step back, although she now wanted John and me to manage everything but retain all the decision-making and financial control herself.

John told her that was not possible as our views were simply too far apart now and either she ran it or we did. In the event, the Thai board stepped in after being told they needed to make a decision. They had also heard rumours that Margot had plans to euthanise all the dogs at the old restaurant and they decided overwhelmingly that they wanted us to take charge and Margot left.

It was a sad time but Margot needed to sort her life out. Once her personal life was in order, she returned to Bangkok and even started a private sterilisation clinic.

We still hear from her occasionally and I think deep down she must be happy to see how Soi Dog has grown. Coincidentally, most of her emails are about helping individual dogs rather than sterilisation so maybe she has also come around to seeing that if you are going to sterilise large numbers of dogs, you are also going to have to find somewhere for dogs that cannot be returned to the street.

Margot rightly gets annoyed when she reads an article in the press describing me or John or both of us as the founders of Soi Dog. Of course, we can't be responsible for what people write and always make it clear, when people ask, how Margot initially started Soi Dog as a one-woman organisation in Bangkok.

She worked phenomenally hard during those first three years, but it was her decision to quit in 2006 when we were still a very small organisation, so unless people read the history on our website it is unlikely that they would know about her, the same as they will forget about John and me in years to come. It is all about the dogs, not the people involved.

If a dog was in trouble, then Margot would do everything humanly possible to help it and would turn out any time day or night to help a dog in distress. Like me, she was no diplomat, though, and I well remember John getting a phone call to say a man had thumped her in the eye. It turned out she'd got into an argument about who should give way on a narrow stretch of road near her house, and rather than just reversing a few yards got into a verbal fight, resulting in her receiving a black eye.

On another occasion, John had to rescue her from the dog pound when she climbed over the gate to get a dog she thought should not be there. The women who worked there were attacking her with sticks, and it turned out the dog belonged to friends of theirs and they were just looking after it until she got back. She would regularly fall out with volunteers and I would have to persuade them to stay, so we were not that different when it came to diplomacy.

Now she was gone, the pressure fell squarely on our shoulders. John was still collecting food every day from hotels and caring for the dogs and cats at temples. I was overseeing the centre and managing the vets and other staff, and in the evenings we would both burn the midnight oil answering all the correspondence and keeping all the paperwork straight. We believed in the personal touch, and every donor deserved a personal reply.

Gradually, yet also rather suddenly, Soi Dog was completely taking over our lives. The animals we were caring for depended on us. The conditions at the building in Phuket Town were far from ideal and we desperately needed somewhere else, but finding suitable land on Phuket, and more importantly the money to buy it or even rent, and then build suitable buildings was beyond our reach at that time.

Our Thai president, however, had an idea. In 2002, the then governor of Phuket, who was, in fact, a dog-lover, had decided to build a shelter for stray dogs on forestry land owned by the government on the main highway, not far away from the airport.

Unfortunately, governors are moved around regularly, and in 2003 when the pound was completed he had already gone and his successor had no interest at all, other than for it to be a place to put stray dogs, and he handed over the responsibility of managing it to the local Department of Livestock Development (DLD), whose role is to ensure meat is up to quality and prevent disease in farm animals. They had no budget to manage it properly and the local authorities were not keen on the idea of supporting it either. With only a couple of not-so-young ladies to keep it clean and feed the dogs, it soon became a mess.

In addition, whoever had designed it had not done a very good job. With a low wall surrounding the main dog enclosure and no proper drainage, the enclosure soon flooded in the rainy season with half of it underwater. In addition, the gap between the wall and the fence above it was too wide to stop smaller dogs crawling through it, and the fence itself was too low to stop bigger, more agile dogs easily climbing over it. The big problem was that the shelter was on a very fast section of the main highway. The section of road stretching a few hundred meters either side of the entrance became a killing field for dogs who found themselves in a strange environment. Of course, many had no experience of dealing with traffic, having lived on beaches all their lives.

The solution, therefore, was that Soi Dog move into the pound, bringing 'our' dogs with us, and carry out the necessary improvements. Although we had always been opposed to the pound, it made sense to try to work with it rather than against it and try to change the authority's approach to dumping dogs there as opposed to us sterilising them.

In 2006, following a fundraising appeal and using all of our available funds, we installed proper drainage, made the fencing totally secure, built and equipped a vet clinic, and split the huge run into three.

We also built a clinic and further smaller buildings to provide separate areas for sick dogs and puppies. We even built an agility course as one of our volunteers was an experienced agility trainer, and it would provide a great diversion for the dogs.

Initially, things went well. The number of volunteers was increasing both locally and overseas. Soi Dog would never have grown into the organisation it is today without its small army of volunteers. Many come and then, finding it starting to take over their lives, leave, but not before making an impact, and I am grateful to them all.

They included people like Sarah Heaney, who was from the UK but lived in Saudi Arabia with her husband, who was working there training pilots. After Margot fell out with her sister in Holland, Sarah took over the website. It was quite basic, but it got the message across and, like everybody else, she was working for nothing.

Alan Archer came not long after we moved into the pound. He helped considerably in building up the number of supporters. Ina from Germany became our first shelter manager. Others helped by organising local fundraisers in Phuket and overseas. It was at this time that people who are still with us to this day, such as Claudia from Switzerland and Cristy who lived on Phuket, first appeared, as did Rob from the US who, with his partner, Mark, was instrumental in setting up Soi Dog United States.

I cannot even attempt to try to remember everyone, so apologies that you are not all named, but without you Soi Dog would never have grown into what it is today.

At one point after the tsunami, Merritt Clifton, who was then editor of the *Animal People* newspaper in the US, came to visit us. He suggested to John that we send him our annual accounts as *Animal People* published an annual report on charities' finances and he said it could help us get donations. John duly sent them off only to get a scathing reply from Merritt pointing out that John had stated 100% of donations were going on programmes and nothing on fundraising or admin.

John told him that that was the case as everything was done by volunteers at their own expense. Merritt strongly advised John that he put some value to his time and include that as donors would not believe 100% was going on programmes, and if they did believe it would consider us unsustainable.

We said too bad, that was the situation, and I like to think one of the reasons people *did* come and help us in those days was because they could see that everything went to the animals and not even expenses were claimed.

We were, of course, fortunate that we had our pensions and savings, and although not wealthy, we did not need anything from Soi Dog. Of course, as we have grown it has been increasingly important to employ more and more staff as not everybody is in our position, but we still pride ourselves on ensuring the maximum possible goes directly to the programmes, and all our boards and activities overseas are still run by volunteers to this day.

Back to the pound, and although things were much better than at the old restaurant, there always seemed to be issues with the DLD. The Phuket director did not like us at all. I assume he looked upon it as a loss of face that Soi Dog was running our part of the pound a lot better than they were running theirs.

Ridiculous statements by him in the press that he was going to remove every dog in Phuket and put them in the pound also led to public spats, as such statements could not go unchallenged.

We believed in CNVR (Capture, Neuter, Vaccinate, Release), not dumping every dog in underfunded, understaffed dog pounds. Removing sterilised vaccinated dogs was having the opposite effect of what everybody wanted: no stray dogs and no rabies. Eventually, he announced that the regional director had stated that it was inappropriate for an NGO to be running a government facility and that we must leave.

The fact that we had provided over three-million-baht-worth of improvements clearly counted for nothing. We could give them money but we could not use the place any longer.

Fortunately, we were able to negotiate a few months' notice and set about on another search.

It was Dr Suchon, who was also on the Soi Dog board, who came to the rescue again. Dr Suchon and his wife, Khun Toom, had helped us from the outset. An incredibly kind man, he was the vet the poor went to, as if they could not afford the treatment he would charge them just a token amount or even nothing at all.

He was apparently the first vet to open a private practice in Bangkok and obviously had private means, as he owned valuable land on Phuket as well as a valuable vintage car collection.

Some of this land was in Mai Khao, including a house they owned. He knew all the local people, of course, and opposite his house was some land which he told us the owner would rent to us on a long lease and at a reasonable rent. Our prayers were answered. The land had a lake on it and at that point was not enclosed. It only had a partially completed two-storey house and open cattle shed, plus a block of four rooms in dire need of repair, but it was big enough, and all we had to do now was raise the money to build the basic runs and an office and clinic …

An urgent appeal was sent out to all our supporters; larger organisations were contacted and local fundraisers held. The race was on. We had said we would be out by the end of March 2008. The open cattle shed was converted into a clinic with a front office and eight brand-new runs were built. Each one is named after the person or group that paid for its construction. The block of four rooms was repaired and had bathrooms fitted to provide accommodation for the carers who would look after the dogs.

On Saturday 8 March 2008, when those volunteers who also worked during the week could help, the big move happened and all our dogs were taken from the pound to Mai Khao. The DLD director had instructed his staff that we were not allowed to take any of the government dogs. We had been sneaking out the most vulnerable into our runs over the previous few weeks. Whether the two ladies noticed or not, I have no idea.

On the day of the move, Alan turned up with a wad of 1000-baht notes, determined to get as many pound dogs out as he could. A bit of bribery can go a long way, but they would only let us buy so many as they knew the director would come up after we had gone and they would be in trouble if too many dogs were gone.

Multiple trips were made to and fro, and eventually as many dogs that could be moved were. The expressions on their faces indicated they were very happy with their new homes. Of course we felt for the other dogs that were in the government section, especially as we were hearing we would not be allowed to go back in, but at least we had got the more vulnerable ones out, as well as all the ones we had rescued.

We had a new home, at least for the next ten years, and a lot could happen in that time. So it proved.

Just Gill

# Battling dog meat trade
## (You can only do as much as the funds you raise)

As Margot had warned, running and maintaining a shelter was expensive, and our sterilisation numbers were hit hard. With a grant from the World Society for the Protection of Animal (WSPA), as it was then known, we were able to sterilise more than 6,000 dogs in 2005 and over 7,000 in 2006, compared with just over 1,200 in 2004.

With money being first focused on the government pound and then the new shelter, it was to be six years before sterilisation numbers passed the 2006 total.

Had we made the right decision? I believe we had, and the sort of numbers we are achieving today is entirely because of the other work we did in the intervening years.

Other than major trusts and a few individuals who understand the underlying issues, most people will not readily donate to having thousands of faceless dogs and cats sterilised. But show them a picture of an animal in desperate need of help and they will donate to save that animal. There is no criticism implied here; it is human nature, and also why I wanted to have a shelter and not just sterilise dogs.

The fact is that since 2012, the reason why we have seen the number of dogs and cats sterilised each year rise – to more than 80,000 in 2018 – is not that people now understand the need for it, but rather that they have trusted us to use their donations wisely. They have seen the thousands of dogs we have saved from horrendous situations, whether individual cases of cruelty, large-scale abuse, or natural disasters.

In effect, it has been getting involved in things outside the core sterilisation programme that has enabled us to sterilise far more dogs than would otherwise have been possible.

As John never tires of saying, 'A charity, however good it is, can only do as much as the funds it raises', which brings us to Leonard.

Between us, John and I and other volunteers all dedicated time to raising money, whether we were writing thank yous or applying for grants, or Cristy running an event, or Alan and Sarah building an improved website.

John was already spending more time on his computer than he was out in the field. A French volunteer called Nadege joined up, and as I recall started our Facebook page. Claudia was spreading the word in Switzerland and other German-speaking countries and Mah was doing the same in the United States.

It is fair to say, though, that love him or hate him, Leonard Coyne did more to accelerate the growth of Soi Dog than anybody before or since, sitting, as he still does, in his office in not quite the Australian outback.

We had received a donation from him and, as usual, John had written a personal thank you which clearly impressed Leonard. It turned out his hobby was rock-climbing and he regularly came to Thailand to climb the limestone formations in Krabi, which was around three hours away from Phuket.

John suggested that on Leonard's next trip he call in to see us as he had to fly to Phuket airport anyway, and that is exactly what he did. He was blown away by what we were doing and determined to try to help more animals.

Leonard's involvement with Soi Dog resulted from an unlikely series of circumstances. In 2010, while travelling in Bhutan, Leonard's wife, Cathy, came across a street dog in dire straits. Suffering from malnutrition and disease, the dog was unlikely to survive the coming winter in the foothills of the Himalayas.

Bringing the dog back to their hotel room and giving her a bath, Cathy promptly ordered her a room service breakfast which she devoured quickly, after which she fell asleep on Leonard's lap.

Fate works in mysterious ways, and at certain junctures in life people often make abrupt decisions which have far-reaching and unexpected consequences. Realising the dog's chance of survival was slim, Leonard decided to take the dog home to Australia. That journey is another story in itself, although you will be pleased to know the mission was successful and Shanti, as she is now known, lives in the lap of luxury.

While researching ways to get Shanti from Bhutan to Australia, Leonard stumbled on Soi Dog's website. As he had spent considerable time rock-climbing in Thailand, the foundation piqued his interest. Soi Dog seemed like a solid organisation and he impulsively made a substantial donation.

To put it simply, Leonard was blown away by what we were doing and determined to try to help us.

He had a background in sales but had never done any fundraising before. Although very different people, we were the same in believing that if you are going to take something on then you either do it right or don't bother at all.

Leonard invested in books and taught himself the basics of how charities attract donors, but more importantly saw the growing phenomenon of Facebook, that up to now charities had largely ignored.

He began to study how Facebook worked and how charities could benefit from it. I don't pretend to understand these things, and, to be honest, Facebook and other social media sites leave me cold, but Leonard did, and before long our following began to grow and to grow rapidly as people began to spread the word about Soi Dog to their friends.

Within a relatively short space of time, our following on Facebook had grown from just a few thousand to over 100,000 and eventually to over a million.

Today, of course, all charities use Facebook and other social media platforms, but in reality it was Leonard that really saw the possibilities that others then followed.

Today, Facebook has changed how it operates and how stories are spread, and it is far harder for charities to benefit from it without investing large sums in advertising, which, of course, is what Facebook wants.

There was no shortage of real-life stories to keep people across the world interested in what was happening to animals in Thailand, and as donations increased we were able to do more to help them. The more animals we helped, the more people supported us.

I was always opposed to paying money out on fundraising, but just as Merritt had pointed out to John years before, Leonard was adamant that if we wanted to see the sort of impact we dreamed of happening, then we had to invest in fundraising.

Grudgingly, I agreed but warned that it would be over my dead body if we ever became like some charities I was aware of where only a few cents in the dollar actually went on helping animals or people.

Back in 2008, John had been sent a copy of a photo that had appeared in the Bangkok Post newspaper. It had been taken in Laos and showed a large truck packed with cages that contained more than 1,500 Thai dogs, it said, on their way to Vietnam to be sold for dog meat.

We had heard rumours that there were restaurants in Chiang Mai selling dog meat, but had never heard of dogs being shipped to Vietnam for this purpose.

John began to look into it and discovered it was a lucrative but illegal trade involving tens of thousands of dogs each year.

Of course, in 2008 we were still small and desperately raising funds to build our shelter. John wrote to every major international animal charity asking if they could intervene and help stop this trade. Most did not even reply, including some which now having seen that the trade brings in funds do solicit donations for it without actually doing anything about it.

The one or two that did reply gave excuses as to why they could not be involved. John did not know it at the time but was to find out later that WSPA had invested a huge sum of money in having a full survey and report done on the dog meat industry in Thailand, but had suppressed it as they considered it too politically sensitive.

Political sensitivity was the reason they gave John why they could not be involved. To their credit, some years later they admitted this and apologised and did release the report, but too late to save hundreds of man hours being wasted on information they already knew. Feeling frustrated and angry, John had to put it out of his mind, but with Leonard on board and us beginning to grow, in 2011 the pair of them began a campaign to target this incredibly cruel trade.

Nobody knows for sure how many dogs (and cats) are brutally killed in Asia each year for their meat and, in some cases, also their fur and skin. If you were to go to a Ministry of Agriculture in any country in Asia, it is likely they could tell you how many cattle or pigs had been slaughtered for their meat each year. Why? Because livestock production is, by and large, controlled to ensure we humans are not poisoned by eating animals produced for our consumption.

Figures relating to the number of dogs and cats slaughtered for meat are pure guesswork. Nowhere in Asia have dogs or cats been classified as livestock, and as a result there are no regulations regarding their use as such.

Estimates vary, but a figure of thirty million dogs per year is often used to estimate the total number of dogs consumed each year throughout Asia, with China being the largest consumer, followed by Vietnam and Korea.

Dogs are also consumed in virtually all other Southeast Asian countries, whether legal or not. No estimates exist for the consumption of domestic cats, which is increasingly popular, particularly in Vietnam.

In no country in Asia, excepting Korea, are dogs commercially farmed, and even in Korea there are currently no controls over those farms, which range from backyard operations to large establishments with hundreds of dogs.

The vast majority of dogs used for dog meat are bought from poor villagers who don't want the excess puppies being produced or dogs that are simply snatched from the streets or people's yards with no regard given to whether they are owned or not.

With no controls, the transportation, handling, and killing of the animals is never humane and at its worst incredibly cruel.

In some areas it is believed that the adrenalin produced when pain is inflicted improves the texture or flavour of the meat. Other myths have been perpetuated by sellers, including, for example, in Cambodia, that black dogs are the best to eat, and in Vietnam that it is good luck to eat dogs at the end of the lunar cycle.

In Vietnam, eating dog meat is most popular in the winter because it is believed it warms the blood. In Korea, it is most popular in the height of summer to combat the effects of the heat.

Many young men believe it enhances strength and is an aphrodisiac, particularly when eaten while drinking beer. Personally, I always thought drinking beer had the opposite effect …

In Thailand, dog meat is consumed in different areas and in different ways. In the area of Chiang Mai and Chiang Rai, eating dogs was mainly practised by the Akha people, a hill tribe that moved into this region of Thailand more than two hundred years ago.

They would eat or sacrifice excess dogs in the same way they would kill and eat other animals. As the Akha grew rich on the proceeds of opium, they have now spread into mainstream Thai society, but old habits die hard, and specialist restaurants sprang up to cater for those wanting dog meat. They could be identified by a black pot hanging outside the door. In one such restaurant, the owner said they only ate bad dogs.

The other main area is Isaan, which is the vast north-eastern region of Thailand that borders Laos. Isaan even has its own language and many people consider themselves as much Lao as they do Thai. It is also the area where Vietnamese refugees fleeing from religious persecution settled, with the town of Tha Rae in Sakhon Nakhon province being populated by mainly Vietnamese and their descendants.

The town boasts a Roman Catholic cathedral and a nunnery and is the capital of the dog meat industry in Thailand. There were also many tanneries in the area processing dog skin, used in the manufacture of musical instruments. The skin from male dogs' scrotums is apparently used in the manufacture of the finest golf gloves owing to the softness and elasticity of the skin.

Dog meat was openly on sale throughout the town. In addition, dog meat has been discovered on sale in items like meat balls in Bangkok, in a similar way to how horse meat was recently discovered in products in Europe.

Dogs are also caught and consumed in smaller numbers throughout the country by migrant workers from the surrounding countries, who make up a large part of Thailand's manual labour and live in large shanty towns close to where they work.

The vast majority of Thais find the thought of eating dog meat abhorrent, but as a tolerant race mostly considered those that did eat it as, in effect, country hicks.

What Thai people in general were not aware of was the growing trade in Thai dogs being sent illegally to Vietnam, nor the cruelty involved in the business. The only reason at that time that the trade was illegal was because of safety laws surrounding the spread of disease, notably rabies, which all Association of Southeast Asian Nations (ASEAN) countries, including Thailand and Vietnam, had pledged to eliminate by 2020.

In 2011, a precedent was set when the then governor of Nakhon Phanom, through which province smugglers were transporting dogs, personally led the interception of trucks containing over a thousand dogs. They were on their way to the Mekong River and to boats to take them over the border and into Laos before a final road journey to Vietnam.

The rescued dogs were taken to the Nakhon Phanom livestock centre, and people donated millions of baht to a fund to care for the dogs. It was clear that many Thai people were as outraged as we were when they learned what was happening.

This is how we began to become actively involved in ending the dog meat trade in Thailand, which the Thai veterinary authorities estimated involved up to 500,000 dogs per year, either killed locally or exported to Vietnam.

The issue caused a big debate with many people, including foreigners, questioning what was wrong with killing and eating stray dogs compared to eating pigs and chickens and other animals.

Surely it was a productive way of keeping numbers down. The first step was, therefore, to educate people about the horrors of the trade.

Everything about it, from capture to final killing, was inhumanity at its worst. Photos and videos were acquired from both within Thailand when trucks were intercepted and Vietnam.

There, dogs were first taken to large holding centres where liquid rice was forcibly pumped into them to increase their weight – and hence their value.

In the actual restaurants, dogs were routinely thrown into vats of boiling water and de-furring machines while still alive. Clubbing dogs to death with an iron bar was the normal way of dispatching, but even this was done in front of the other dogs who clearly understood what fate awaited them.

Everything, of course, was about money, and the more dogs that could be transported per crate, the better. Iron cages too small for a person to get into were stuffed with dogs, often ten or more per crate. Often limbs would be stuck out and the heavy cages were piled one on top of the other. Many legs were crushed, and often dogs in the lower rows would suffocate on the long journey. You could argue these were the lucky ones.

Films were produced to show the Thai people what was going on. In addition, we made films to show the world what was happening.

A video we called *I Didn't Know*, featuring Ricky Gervais and Dame Judi Dench, as well as other stars of stage and screen, had a particular impact, and it became clear that people were behind stopping this horror.

Ella Todd of Environment Films and her husband, Ben, donated their time in making the film, and the wonderful actor Peter Egan got the other stars involved.

Ella had previously visited us to make a short promo film which ended up being a full blown one-hour documentary, again at no cost as she was so impressed with what we were trying to do. That film is a bit of history now but can still be seen on YouTube.

In addition, we offered rewards to the police and other law enforcement agencies on the border for arrests made, based on prosecutions and number of dogs saved. People may think such payments encourage corruption. The fact is that corruption among the people responsible for enforcing the law on the border was rife, and they were ignoring the smugglers and even warning them of possible raids.

It was not easy for them. Many lived among communities that were heavily involved in smuggling and in that part of Thailand, getting permanently rid of somebody was not difficult to do. In addition, the pay of a policeman is very small, and it is almost accepted that they need to supplement their incomes.

This was a war, and we needed to encourage those police and Thai Navy officers willing to stand up against the mafia, who controlled not only the dog smuggling but also trafficking of wildlife and illegal timber, drugs, and even children.

At the same time, the Thai youth in particular were demonstrating in Bangkok, demanding the authorities do more, and calls for an animal welfare bill became stronger.

Other societies also began to see the public mood and were willing to cooperate. Animals Asia, who although focusing on bears in China were also active in Vietnam, joined us and two other organisations in an alliance to try to persuade the governments of Thailand, Vietnam, Laos, and Cambodia to ban the movement of dogs across their borders, based entirely on the threat such movements posed to the spread of rabies.

Although resistant at first, the Vietnamese authorities, who were the lead nation in the efforts to eliminate the disease throughout the region, could not argue with the logic that John and others put to them in meetings in Hanoi and Bangkok – namely that if they wanted to end rabies, as they professed to be trying to do, then that would never happen while they allowed rabies-infected dogs to enter the country illegally. The result was that they imposed a five-year ban on the import of dogs across Vietnamese borders.

The other governments pledged to do all in their power to stop the trade at source. Whether the ban would be implemented remained to be seen, but we now began producing large posters on the Vietnamese side of the border crossings with Laos, where dogs had traditionally crossed, warning that it was now illegal.

In addition, a media campaign including a Vietnamese version of the *I Didn't Know* video was started in Vietnam, utilising the support of popular Vietnamese entertainers to change public attitudes to dog meat there and show the cruelty involved. Over a million young Vietnamese people signed the petition.

Pressure increased on the smugglers and thousands of dogs were intercepted in Thailand, including one interception of nearly two thousand dogs in a holding centre on the outskirts of Tha Rae.

Nakhon Phanom was already full to bursting and other livestock centres were used to house the dogs. Of those two thousand dogs intercepted in Tha Rae, more than six hundred never arrived at their destination of Buriram, and the remainder were found to have all disappeared a few months later, leading to accusations of dogs being sold back to the traders by the authorities.

Whatever the truth, it was clear that more needed to be done to help the intercepted dogs, and we embarked on a campaign to build a huge shelter at Buriram as well as improving the others at Nakhon Phanom, Mukdaharn, and Thong Pha Phum.

The costs of caring for the dogs were huge, but we were holding onto the belief that smugglers were only in it for money and they must now be losing large amounts with so many dogs being intercepted and, hopefully, the Vietnamese authorities refusing them entrance into Vietnam.

Financially, it made no sense for them to continue smuggling dogs, which could be spotted so easily. Smuggling timber and wildlife was sadly far more profitable and less risky, although I am happy to say that some of our operations also led to the interception of large shipments of illegal wildlife.

In terms of the law, this was still based on disease control, not cruelty. Thailand had no meaningful animal welfare laws. A local Thai organisation, the TSPCA, had spent years trying to have a very basic law introduced, which, although a start, even if it was passed had little bite to it and no mention of dog meat being banned.

Other Thai organisations, notably the Thai Animal Guardians Association, were not happy and wanted a stronger law. Then, in 2014, an event occurred that surprisingly would, as it turned out, have a positive impact: the military coup.

Now, I am not in favour of military coups, but I have to say that the military regime in Thailand has done more to fight corruption than any democratically elected government had for years.

They were also keen to push through some of the bills that had been lying on the statute books. Through influential Thai contacts, John was able to meet with some of the generals who were now running the country, and with the assistance of Thai activists, the animal welfare bill became one of those that the regime decided to push through Parliament.

A committee was formed to review the bill, and John campaigned long and hard to have the killing of animals classified as domestic pets illegal, except by a veterinarian. This, of course, included the dog meat industry.

He also campaigned successfully to have the maximum punishments for offenders doubled to two years in prison and/or a 40,000-baht fine. He is one of the few foreigners invited to address the Thai Parliament on any subject. Although the animal welfare law in Thailand requires a lot more work and clarification, it is a start and has led to the criminalisation of killing dogs and cats for meat in Thailand.

Of course, making something illegal does not mean that there are not plenty of people happy to break the law. The Mekong River forms a border between Thailand and Laos stretching for several hundred kilometres, and for local people it is virtually an open border, with long-tail boats crisscrossing it along its entire length.

Local people continue to smuggle odd dogs across the river, mainly for consumption at Laos dog meat restaurants, and we continue to find local butchers still plying their trade. The days of tens of thousands of dogs going to Vietnam in large trucks are, at least for now, over.

Considering we never expected to see it happen in our lifetimes, the operation, which lasted three years, was a huge success.

Today, we continue to work on ending the dog meat trade universally, but of course this is not easy and every country is different.

In Thailand, we continue to support undercover teams and offer rewards to those who uncover now illegal acts of killing dogs for meat. We have had posters made in Khmer, Vietnamese, Lao, and Burmese and are erecting them in the areas where migrant workers from these countries are known to be snatching dogs for meat.

Outside of Thailand, our focus today is on Korea, where we focus more on changing the attitude of the Korean people through advertising and supporting local groups, and Vietnam, where, as with the rest of Asia, the increase in pet ownership is seeing a change in attitude.

In addition, tests carried out on dogs killed in slaughterhouses in Hanoi show a significant number infected with rabies.

It may not be easy to convince Vietnamese authorities to ban dog meat based on the cruelty issue, but the risks involved in eating meat over which no controls exist are very high, and outbreaks of cholera, for example, have been linked directly to dog meat.

The biggest driver for change, though, is the local people, particularly the young and educated who are becoming far more environmentally aware than their fathers and mothers and are starting to campaign for change themselves.

We, as foreigners, should focus on supporting their efforts. Trying to change things by telling a person they are evil and wrong isn't the answer; this can and does have the opposite effect to that which was intended.

Many Koreans who have never tasted dog meat and may privately disagree with it will defend it because they see it as foreigners attacking their culture. They quite rightly ask what the reaction would be in the West if Asians began protesting outside McDonald's demanding an end to killing cows.

Of course, no culture should involve cruelty. Should dogs be treated differently when it comes to food? Surprisingly, we receive more criticism from vegans than we do from meat-eaters regarding ending the dog meat trade. Most of the criticism is based on why we don't campaign against eating all animals.

The obvious answer is, of course, in our name. We are a dog foundation working to end the suffering of stray dogs, and although we support other causes, as a foundation our mission is very clear.

There are many groups campaigning for farm animals, and they do not and neither would I expect them to suddenly start campaigning to help stray dogs.

It is also important to remember that originally dogs were never bred by man to be food and in no country are dogs or domestic cats classified as livestock.

In times of famine and desperation people will eat anything, even other people, but whereas pigs, sheep, cattle, and other livestock animals were created, rightly or wrongly, by man from wild animals for the sole purpose of providing food, dogs were bred by man originally from the wolf to provide protection for his livestock and home.

Over the years, many different breeds were developed to perform different tasks, but no breed was developed as a source of food. In relatively recent times we have bred dogs to be companions more than anything else.

We have created a domestic animal from a pack animal and turned something that survived by hunting into something that can no longer survive without our help. In my opinion we have a duty to that animal. The reason there are so many stray dogs and cats is because of our irresponsibility. Persecuting them because of our irresponsibility is hypocrisy in the extreme.

The other reason why we campaign against dog meat is that there are no controls. Carnivorous animals cannot be farmed humanely, and even though I am not naïve enough to believe that the slaughter of livestock across the world is always carried out humanely, and know that factory farming is inherently cruel, the transportation and killing of dogs is cruelty at its worst because there are no controls at all.

I personally do not eat meat and would be delighted to see all meat consumption end, but for now we are focusing on dogs, and if we can get people to question the eating of dogs, surely they will also start to question the eating of all living creatures. Certainly, the growth in vegetarianism and veganism in the West is an indicator that this is happening, and many of our supporters are vegan or vegetarian.

I would like to think that at least some of them have been influenced because of what we have revealed about cruelty to man's best friend.

Armchair activists who waste our time by demanding answers to inane questions should get off their backsides and actually do something about it themselves if they care so much.

It's the same with people who ask us why we waste our time on animals and don't help children instead.

I have never come across one of them who is actually doing anything themselves to make a difference, or in fact is actually doing anything themselves to make a difference to anything.

Had we not moved to Phuket, where the stray dog problem was so bad with nobody doing anything much about it, but had moved somewhere else where there was a much bigger problem, then the chances are we would now be involved in something entirely different.

Our biggest private donor started supporting us after spending several months here and seeing what we were doing and how we were tackling it. He had previously worked in West Africa, where he set up a very successful charity fighting malaria. In our experience, people who help animals are also the first to answer human crises as well. It is not about helping animals or people.

While on the subject of food, I don't think it is as simple as people make out. I saw recently in an email from a vegan organisation a chart showing the lifespan of an animal bred for food compared with its natural lifespan. Surely that is irrelevant? If nobody ate meat then these animals would not exist, except perhaps in a few petting zoos to show people what we humans used to eat.

Every farmer would have to have all his animals killed and switch to production of other foods, in the same way that, sadly, activists have to realise that if Korea made dog meat illegal tomorrow, the two-million-plus dogs in farms could not all be rehomed.

Hens would also no longer exist, unless as pets, which would have to be sterilised or their eggs destroyed or you would be overrun with unwanted chickens, same as you would be overrun with kittens and puppies if you did nothing to stop them breeding.

People who have a vision of fields full of grazing sheep and cows that are no longer being used for meat or dairy products and able to live a natural life are, quite frankly, living in cloud cuckoo land.

If these fields were turned over to the production of grains, cereals, and vegetables, then there is no doubt that we would be able to produce far more food to feed the world's growing population, and far more efficiently and cheaper, but people would have to accept that all animals that are currently used just for food production or clothing would have to be destroyed.

Wildlife would hopefully prosper, of course, though steps would have to be taken to prevent wild animals destroying crops meant for human consumption.

Of course, the issue today is that although more and more people in the West are choosing to adopt a vegetarian or vegan lifestyle, in other parts of the world where traditionally little meat was eaten, demand is increasing as personal wealth grows, so factory farming explodes as the quest to produce more meat at lower prices continues.

Back to the dog meat issue – isn't it strange how those big organisations that wanted nothing to do with it back in 2008 are now campaigning like mad when they see how prospective donors in the West are interested in the topic?

Just like with disasters, most actually do very little other than point out what people already know. The problem is they can do more harm than good.

The Chinese city of Yulin has become the target in recent years, with virtually every animal organisation I can think of appealing for funds to do what? What people don't realise is that Yulin is a large city in one of the Chinese provinces where dog meat is eaten widely.

It has, I am informed, more than 170 restaurants specialising in dog meat that are open year-round, and markets that support them and private consumers.

In an effort to boost business, local traders introduced the dog meat festival as part of a lychee festival in 2009, which is held every year for ten days at the end of June.

Following widespread publicity and opposition, both within China and beyond, the local government of Yulin publicly announced that the festival no longer existed as a sponsored event and banned all government employees from attending.

The festival *did* continue, and both Chinese and international activists continued to attend. Large numbers of dogs were brought to the festival for the express purpose of selling them at inflated prices to these activists, who were bringing in huge sums of money from supporters to save the dogs. Sadly, the majority of these dogs later died in squalid shelters.

That Yulin raised awareness of the dog meat issue is very true, although there are many in the West who believe that dog meat begins and ends at Yulin because of the huge press coverage it has received.

That the protests have led to its demise is great, but buying dogs from dog meat traders sadly does nothing to stop the industry. As hard as it is to see live dogs for sale, if you buy one another will take its place.

It is the same with the current trend of buying dogs from Korean dog meat farms in return for promises that the farmer will do something else instead, and then shipping those dogs to the United States and other countries, where many sadly end up being euthanised.

It may bring in large donations, but the Korean dog meat industry is an economic business, driven, like any other, by supply and demand. There is no doubt that demand is falling, and as such many of the estimated 17,000 farms will close as the price is driven down.

If demand increases then buying out the odd farm will do nothing to reduce the number of dogs killed, as other farms will increase production or new ones open.

Dog meat will end through the will of the people in the countries where it is consumed and by the lawmakers of those countries.

Great progress is now being made in Korea by activists and politicians to end the dog meat industry there, but as with eating meat generally, we will have to accept that the farmers be given time to switch to other businesses or accept large-scale euthanasia of the dogs.

There is definitely a case, for example, in the Philippines, where it is illegal to organise the interception of dogs destined for consumption and to do as we did in Thailand and pay rewards and rescue the dogs, but first you must have legislation on your side.

Taiwan, through the efforts of Hong Kong billionaire Genlin and his organisation World Dog Alliance, has now banned dog meat consumption, and there is talk of the Indonesian government doing the same.

Just Gill

# Bangkok floods rescue
## (It never rains but it pours)

Just as things were hotting up with our war against the Thai dog meat trade, in October 2011 the floods that had been affecting the northern provinces in July hit Bangkok with devastating effect. Economically, it is listed as the fourth costliest natural disaster in history, although how much of it was natural and how much down to decisions made by the then government is debatable.

The fact was that large areas of greater Bangkok were underwater. John was in the UK visiting his mother when the news struck but organised for two of our volunteers, Cindy and her husband, Derek, to go up there to see how we could help.

Cindy was an accomplished photographer and had been doing great work at increasing adoptions back in Phuket. It was clear that the situation for large numbers of dogs and cats was critical.

John went straight to Bangkok on his return and, along with Cindy and Derek, was literally working around the clock, organising things on the ground during the day and emailing what was required back to Leonard at night.

The bravery and fortitude of many Thais came to the fore in the subsequent weeks, particularly young women such as Khun Toon and Khun Bee, who would carry out their regular jobs during the day and then immediately go out rescuing dogs in the evening and well into the night, as well as weekends.

John met another young woman, Khun Kharn, who volunteered to act as John's assistant and manage our reception centre, which was an unused showroom on Sukhumvit Soi 71 that the owner loaned us.

In some places it was just a question of getting food to dogs and cats that were stranded and on the roofs and balconies of abandoned houses. The Department of Livestock had set up centres where owners could bring their pets, but of course the street dogs and cats were left to fend for themselves. Fortunately, there were plenty of good-natured people who were willing to give food to the dogs if it could be provided, so distributing food became one of our main functions.

Dogs and cats that were totally isolated and marooned had to be picked up, but obviously did not realise that we were trying to help them. Many were not willing to be rescued, so nets on poles became the main tool in catching them.

We had purchased simple flat-bottomed plastic boats, and good-natured people in Phuket had loaned us outboard motors, though often the volunteers, including John and Derek, had to resort to jumping in the water to push the boats along.

In addition, Edwin Wiek from the Wildlife Friends of Thailand charity near Hua Hin had a large steel boat which he readily made available to rescuers. The Bangkok-based Soi Cat and Dog Rescue, which was still in operation then, had been loaned unaffected land south of the city and set up a temporary shelter there in conjunction with the Chiang Mai-based Elephant Nature Reserve, which was to take many of the rescued dogs from there as they had a large area of land connected to their elephant sanctuary.

Edwin also had spare land in Hua Hin and an animal hospital on site. We provided the materials to build a temporary dog shelter and got volunteer vets to sterilise and treat the dogs we sent there.

By far the biggest single operation was at Phuttamonthon Buddhist Park. This is a huge park on the outskirts of Bangkok, which is the centre of Buddhism in Thailand.

As they don't want stray dogs wandering all over the park, a shelter had been built in one corner, and an elderly lady looked after the three to four hundred dogs that lived there.

Unfortunately, the whole park became a vast lake with just small islets of higher ground and the higher part of a small road bridge which crossed one of the canals winding its way through the park. The shelter itself was completely underwater with just bits of roof visible. The dogs had, in the main, moved to the small section of bridge where the old lady was now living with them. Volunteers were bringing food, but it was clear that many of the dogs were sick and with that sort of overcrowding, it would not be long before disease swept through them.

Other dogs would swim from a small islet to and from the bridge, and there were large crocodiles in the water, for which these dogs were easy prey. The problem was that to the nearest road was a good twenty minutes by boat, and it took nearly four hours to get there from our centre in Bangkok, plus we had small boats which could only carry a few dogs at a time.

I had joined John by this time, and although I was not going to be that much use, as metal prosthetic legs and water do not get on well, I could provide treatment to sick dogs on the bridge.

The decision was made that if we were going to save these dogs then they all would need evacuating. The first priority was to get the really sick ones off and get them to a vet in Bangkok near our centre. That was the easy part, but what about the others?

John asked Edwin if he could build a bigger temporary shelter. Edwin does not mess about and, with Soi Dog providing the finance, was able to build a large open pen into which separate smaller pens lined with bales of straw and covered with tarpaulins to keep them dry were built.

Getting the dogs was still going to be a challenge, though. Step in the Thai military. The army had been heavily involved in evacuation operations for weeks, but this was the first time they had been asked to help evacuate over three hundred dogs.

A wonderful colonel took charge, and with his boats and troops and our volunteers in our boats, the operation began. We brought dozens of collapsible cages to the site and rented two large open-backed trucks and a crane. Because so many of the dogs had to be caught and due to the length of time it took to ferry the cages backwards and forwards, it took two days to complete the operation, but at the end of it not one dog remained.

Permits had to be given to the truck drivers as, not surprisingly, they were afraid they would be stopped and arrested as dog smugglers. So that is how the dogs of Phuttamonthon were rescued. They stayed at Edwin's facility for several months as not only was Phuttamonthon one of the last areas to become dry again, major repairs had to be done to the shelter before the dogs could be moved back. One of the happiest outcomes was that all the seriously sick dogs recovered, and with Cindy promoting them for adoption, all found lovely new homes around the world.

We arranged for the old lady who had been their carer to go and visit the dogs, and she continued to look after them until retiring last year. Soi Dog has never forgotten the dogs there and recently carried out major improvements to the shelter.

Not long after the floods were over, the Soi Cat and Dog Rescue (SCAD) asked us if we would take over their operation in Bangkok. The founder had moved and most of the other volunteers did not want to have to deal with the everyday issues of running a charity. We agreed but then the Thai board of SCAD began to impose ridiculous conditions on us. In effect, SCAD would remain with the same staff and we would be contractors and apply to them for grants, when in reality they were almost bankrupt and had no sustainable fundraising policy. We had to back away and, not surprisingly, it closed down shortly afterwards.

Meanwhile, Margot had moved back to Bangkok and opened up a private sterilisation clinic in a large rented house there with the aim that it would be self-financing and carry out sterilisations at cost price.

The house had unfortunately been put out of commission during the floods, but afterwards she asked John if we would be interested in taking it on and buying her equipment. With SCAD closed and a need for sterilisation facilities in Bangkok this made sense, and Soi Dog Bangkok was born.

Yet again out of something bad (the floods) something good happened.

Kharn, who had volunteered during the floods, became our first manager in Bangkok, and Toon, who was involved in real estate, began to organise local fundraising.

For John and Leonard and most of the rest of the team, with the floods over it was back to the dog meat trade, but we and other local groups had learned that we could cope with a natural disaster on our doorstep.

During the floods, we once again witnessed large international organisations fundraising but doing hardly anything practical to help. Both Edwin's Wildlife Friends of Thailand and Soi Dog resigned as member societies of WSPA, which had even asked Edwin for use of his boat to give a prospective major donor a tour of the city and take it away from the relief work it was doing.

The total sum of their aid ran to a few tons of dog food. Not long afterwards, WSPA announced it was changing its name and doing away with member societies altogether.

I have already mentioned that our core mission of sterilisation had suffered as focus was put on what seemed to be never-ending emergencies. Unless you can tackle the underlying problem of too many stray dogs fighting over too little food, then the suffering which could be seen everywhere was never going to end.

Many well-meaning local people would devote their lives to going around feeding stray dogs and cats in their neighbourhoods and beyond but had no money to sterilise the dogs or treat them when they were injured or became sick.

Nature did her part, with highly infectious diseases such as distemper and parvovirus periodically wiping out many of the dogs slowly and painfully. Ticks began to multiply and soon were everywhere in Phuket. It was a rare sight to find any dog not infested with them. They, too, began to spread blood parasites from dog to dog, which would slowly kill them if not treated. Some dogs lived for years with such parasites; others went downhill rapidly as the parasites destroyed their red blood cells.

If there is one living creature I take great pleasure in killing, it is the tick. They are a remarkable creature, neither an insect nor a spider; they can lay dormant for years before dropping onto a host that happens to pass by.

I first saw a tick when holidaying in the Lake District in England. I had never seen anything like it and that was just one on Max. In Thailand, a dog could have clumps of thousands on it, and they would go deep into the ears and between the paws. Removing them manually was a slow and laborious process, normally carried out when dogs were asleep from anaesthetic after being sterilised.

Trying to kill the ticks by squeezing them between your fingers or stamping on them rarely worked. We would drop them into bottles of alcohol, and, apologies, but it gave me great pleasure to kill them. Flea and tick collars worked for a while but were expensive, and ivermectin injections or tablets also worked initially but had to be repeated regularly. It also seemed that the ticks were developing immunity to some of the products.

Today, we have Bravecto, which is administered orally in the form of a chew, so you have to have a dog willing to take it from you or be able to force feed it, but it has amazing results. Although there is a Facebook page calling for its ban because of the apparent link between it and some deaths of pets, we have never seen that occur.

Even at places like the government dog pound, where every dog was infested and the walls covered with the things, within days of giving the dogs Bravecto, they disappear as if by magic. Although it is recommended to repeat every three months, with our own dogs we have gone a year before repeating and still not seen a tick. In addition, every dog we sterilise we now vaccinate against distemper and parvo, as well as other common diseases and, of course, rabies. As a result, stray dogs are now living longer, and the need for us to reduce numbers becomes greater.

By 2012, we owned the shelter following successful appeals and were able to develop it slowly in the knowledge that nobody could take it away. Separate areas for puppies and special-needs dogs were built and a badly needed separate cat hospital constructed, as well as staff accommodation to house our mainly Burmese workers who cared for the animals.

But the underlying problem of sterilising all the dogs had to now take priority if we were ever going to solve the issue of too many stray dogs. The sterilisations we did were all done at the shelter and our dog-catchers would go out and bring animals in from many different areas of Phuket.

This was both inefficient and of limited impact. What was needed was a far more targeted and efficient approach involving the local community. What better way than to go back to how it all started: mobile clinics.

The renowned Dogs Trust in Britain had recently started supporting international initiatives with the stray dog problem in the UK now under control, and they were approached to see if they would be interested in supporting such a programme – and they were. So it was that the Phuket PUP (Prevent Unwanted Puppies) programme was born.

The approach was quite simple, and we forecast that it would take three years to complete. The team would consist of two vets, two nurses, two teams of dog catchers, and a manager (me). If we had extra volunteers then we could increase the size of the team. Yes, I was going back to what I loved doing most: hands-on sterilising dogs.

There was only one problem. Personally, the worst thing for me when I lost my legs was also losing my independence. I'd always had my own car in the UK, and even in Thailand I would drive our car while John would drive a truck as he was always carrying dogs and food around. Losing my legs changed all that, and although John or Tris, our gardener, would always drive me where I wanted to go, it was not the same. For a while I tried to drive our car myself as it was an automatic, but on one occasion my right foot became stuck under the brake pedal and I only just narrowly avoided an accident. Killing or injuring myself was one thing, but I could not risk killing somebody else.

John, bless him, came up with a solution. He had been looking at importing disabled controls when, to his amazement, he found a company in Bangkok run by disabled people that specialised in converting cars.

I picked a small red Ford Fiesta and was able to order it in Bangkok. The car was taken to the company, which converted it remarkably cheaply and shipped it down to Phuket.

The conversion was very simple but very effective, and after a few hours driving up and down the road on our estate, I soon got the hang of it.

The controls consisted of a lever attached to the central bulkhead and that had linkages attached to the accelerator and brake pedals. Pull the lever back and the car accelerated, push it forward and it braked. Independent again!

I can't tell you the feeling this gave me. I could go where I wanted, when I wanted and, more importantly, manage the mobile clinics without having to rely on others.

Back in the UK I'd owned a sports car and used to love racing men from traffic lights and waving to them through my window. My racing days might have been over, but if John and I left the shelter at the same time, we would inevitably race each other home and more often than not I would win.

Irresponsible I know, but it made me feel normal again.

Anyway, back to the mobile clinics. Phuket has seventeen separate administrative areas, and we would work systematically starting in the north, moving southwards. Each area, or Or Bor Tor, as they are called in Thai, had its own mayor and other departments such as public health. Obviously, some of the Or Bor Tors were more highly populated than others and had more dogs, but on average we would spend six weeks in each at different locations to make it easy for people to bring their dogs to us, and our dog-catchers would get the strays.

The focus at this time was very much on dogs as nobody saw the cats as a problem, and they were not persecuted like the dogs.

John had forecast, years before, that we could control the dog population, but that while there was such a plentiful food supply, then something was going to eat it, and the island could expect to see an explosion in the feral cat and wild monkey populations, which today is the case.

Control the cats, he said, which is far harder, and expect to see an explosion in rats and mice and snakes which prey on them.

The main reason that stray animals have largely disappeared from wealthier Western nations is simply because of good waste control and the explosion in the acceptance of spaying and neutering pets.

In the UK, for example, what waste is available is now generally taken by wildlife that has moved into the cities. Every household has large dog-proof bins. I am sure in years to come that will be the case in Thailand, but for now the control of waste is appalling and local people think nothing of throwing garbage out of car windows. What dustbins there are are not dog proof.

As for the PUP programme, the plan was to involve the community by organising meetings with the local officials weeks before the clinics in their area actually started. All we required from them were suitable locations that had shelter, light, electricity, water, and a bathroom for the staff.

In addition, they were asked to produce banners in Thai to advertise the clinics and to use their broadcasting system to alert people to them once they had started.

Larger villages and towns generally have loudspeakers on the streets through which the local authority can announce such things.

In more rural areas trucks would go around broadcasting. In addition, at that time the authorities had a budget for rabies vaccines and were expected to provide vaccinations to owners who registered their dogs. It made sense to link this to the clinics.

To tempt owners to have their dogs sterilised, not only did we offer the service for free, we also offered a full vaccination that included distemper and other canine diseases, not just the rabies vaccine the local authority would give.

The meetings were also an opportunity to explain the principles of CNVR to the local officials. Removing vaccinated and sterilised dogs was actually creating a problem, not solving one. They needed to understand this and not expect to see overnight results. Were our words landing on deaf ears? I don't know, but when we started a clinic in Patong at the garbage truck depot, there was even a truck apparently waiting to take the dogs we sterilised immediately away to the dog pound. I made it very clear we would not start the clinic until they went away.

Khun Toom called the mayor's office, and shortly afterwards the truck drove off not to appear again, but we know, of course, that most of the local authorities continue to collect dogs and dump them, either at the pound or in some cases in remote areas in the next province.

What they can't seem to grasp is that if the dogs on the street are all vaccinated and sterilised, then they cannot produce more. Dogs are territorial and will guard their food source. Take them away then others will move in from areas we have not yet fully covered and the whole cycle starts again. It is one of – if not the most – frustrating things we have to deal with. The other is owners who refuse to allow us to sterilise their dogs for a variety of reasons. Some believe it is simply wrong to interfere with nature, others actually want the dogs to have puppies as think they can sell them, others are fearful that the dogs might die under surgery, and others that, particularly male, dogs will no longer be protective of the home.

We can shoot all these arguments down in flames, but still people refuse and generally just dump resulting puppies on the streets and even at times in sacks on the main road on the basis that they have not killed them, but the car or truck that runs over them has. If they survive it is Buddha's will. If anybody can ever explain the logic in that, please do.

Another reason we sometimes heard was in relation to male dogs at temples. Some monks believed the dogs were former monks who had misbehaved and therefore did not want them castrating, presumably in case they also came back as a temple dog. Now that I *could* understand.

The reality is that it is far more important to get the females. You never get every dog, and it only takes one male to impregnate every female in a wide area.

It was hard, exhausting work and played havoc with my stumps, but I loved it and even got to go out with the dog-catchers whenever I could to catch and bring dogs back.

I was away early morning to late evening. Weekends, I would prepare meals for John for the week ahead but insist on a takeaway or eating at a local restaurant on Friday and Saturday nights.

The team had a great spirit and we were averaging over the target of forty dogs per day, often working well after it got dark.

In the south of the island we would stay over Monday to Thursday, as it made no sense to drive all the way back home every night to catch some sleep and then drive all the way back again the following morning. Every time we broke our record there would be high fives and I would treat the team to a special lunch the next day.

And it was working. Over the previous five years we had averaged just over four thousand sterilisations a year, a figure many would be proud of.

In 2012, although the programme did not start until May, we did nearly 10,700, and every year since then has seen numbers increase. In 2018, we sterilised more than 80,000 animals in Thailand, which John believes is more animals than any other organisation is doing anywhere in the world.

Although there is no doubt that vaccinating more than seventy percent of the dog population in an area or country against rabies will all but eliminate the disease, applying the same statistic to stray dog and cat populations, as many organisations do, is not the same.

Similarly, where organisations quote that one pair of cats or dogs can exponentially produce millions in a few years is rubbish. Mathematically it is correct, but any area will only support the number of animals that the food supply available will support, which is why waste food control is so important in controlling numbers. In reality, once the limit is reached, any more puppies or kittens will die of starvation, disease, or be killed by the dominant males.

It is just the same with human beings, as can be seen in the terrible famines in Africa in recent times.

In terms of sterilising, then sterilising seventy or eighty percent of a population is a great start and you will likely see an initial fall in numbers, but picture an island with food source for, say, a thousand dogs. Sterilise eight hundred of them and that still leaves two hundred unsterilised, and for sure a few of their offspring will survive.

As the older sterilised dogs die off, then these few will gradually multiply to take their places. Am I saying we are wasting our time? No, but an ongoing maintenance programme is going to be needed, especially when, as in Phuket, some owners refuse to sterilise their animals and hundreds of puppies are brought in for selling at markets and pet shops every year.

Unsold puppies are inevitably dumped. Even worse, many of these puppies are coming from puppy farms in rabies-endemic areas which pose a risk of introducing the disease to the province.

If you want to bring a dog to Thailand from the rabies-free UK, for example, you will only be allowed in if you can show full vaccination record, health certificate signed by a government-approved vet, and your dog is identified with a microchip.

This is totally correct, of course, and applies to all countries across the world, but you want to bring a dog or puppy from a rabies-endemic area of Thailand to Phuket, which has been rabies free for several years, and nobody will stop you. Crazy or what?

I love the Thai people, but some of their thinking, particularly by those who should know better, can drive you crazy. Many owners in Thailand give their female dogs a contraceptive pill, which all vets know is dangerous and banned in most countries. It is cheap, but invariably the dog develops pyometra, which will lead to death.

We see many female dogs we sterilise that have the disease, and usually when we ask the owner, they confirm they have been giving those tablets. The vets must know yet still prescribe, and some local authorities even give them away. Many Thai vets are totally opposed to terminating pregnancies, even though they know that the resultant puppies are being born into an uncertain future on the streets.

What I can't understand is when they are mid-operation and find that there are foetuses inside the dog they are operating on. They will literally sew the dog back up again, even though it is highly probable they will die inside the mother owing to the anaesthetic getting into their blood streams.

If, as often happens, the mother cannot pass the dead foetuses, then they will rot inside her and she will likely die as well.

Soi Dog will only employ vets who are willing to terminate pregnancies and euthanise dogs that are suffering and have no chance of recovery or quality of life. We will spare no expense in treating them if they are treatable, but will not keep an animal alive because it offends some people to end the life of a suffering creature early. I feel the same way about human euthanasia.

I recall us finding a cat with half its face destroyed, we guessed from a recent road accident. We took her to Dr Trethep's surgery, but sadly he admitted the injuries were too severe for him to be able to deal with. It could be worth trying another vet we knew who was very much a cat expert. The only thing with her was that she would keep terminally ill animals until they died in her surgery as she believed this was the correct thing to do as a devout Buddhist.

Sadly, she said the cat was beyond hope but it could stay in a cage with her until it died. I thanked her very much but said I could do that and would take her home. I actually took her straight back to Dr Trethep, who put her to sleep. If I go to hell for doing such things, so be it. I will not let an animal suffer unnecessarily.

At the same time, people must understand that euthanasia translates as a painless mercy killing. John was attending a conference on the dog meat trade and got talking with the vet, who was then the head of the livestock department in Chiang Mai, about euthanasia and the fact that it was not practised in Thailand by most vets, even when an animal was really suffering and had no chance of recovery.

The vet proudly advised that they did sometimes euthanise dogs, but mainly in market areas where the dogs posed a risk to hygiene. John asked what method they used. She responded proudly that it was very easy: all they did was put some poison, usually strychnine, in some meat and spread it around the area and the dogs would eat it and then go to sleep. The reality, of course, is that such poisoning is not euthanasia as it is neither painless nor merciful for the victim, who will die a slow, agonising death.

The same method is known to be used widely in Thailand, including Phuket, and even in some shelters. Again, it comes back to the perpetrator not physically killing the animal, humanely or not. The dog chooses to eat the baited meat. It's important to note that in most areas, the spreading of it is random and can affect wildlife just as much as the targeted animal.

One of my own dogs, Scooby, was the runt of a litter of nine puppies in Patong. The mother and the other eight were all killed one night eating poisoned bait. Scooby was too weak to reach it and was the sole survivor as a result.

This is one of the most frustrating and difficult aspects of working here, and what led us to looking to establish Soi Dog International.

Just Gill

# Going global

If you had suggested to John or me back in 2003, when there was just the two of us and Margot, that ten years later we would be the largest foundation in Asia working with stray animals, we would have said you were off your rocker, but that was what had happened.

One of the biggest issues –if not *the* biggest issue – of us being a Thai foundation was just that: being a Thai foundation. Our work was nearly all in Thailand, and although we had started supporting projects in other countries, only around five percent of our income was raised here. We had seen other foundations and groups started by foreigners, such as SCAD in Bangkok, close down as the founders left the country or it had become too much for them to cope with any more.

Besides SCAD we had had other groups ask us to take over, but in effect we would be just taking over the exact problems that had led them to quit.

Obviously, John and I were not going to be around forever and having given up our later lives to building the foundation up did not want to see it close when we went.

Each year since turning sixty-four, John had said he would retire on his next birthday, and for sure it would be nice to spend some time together and do those other things we had always planned; seeing the rest of Thailand and the other countries in the region would be a good start.

My only regret is that we were never able to spend the time together I had wished for, but the growth of SDF and the increasing demands this put on us made any life outside of the dogs impossible.

To me this was a calling, and it was unthinkable for us to just dabble at it. It has to be all or nothing.

But finding people who had both the time and were as crazy as we were to take over was not easy, and no way could we turn our backs on the animals.

John Higgs, an expat living in the south of the island, was giving every minute he could spare to helping us, but he still had a business to run and was the first to admit he could not give a hundred percent of his time at the moment.

We needed to find a way to secure the future. We were fortunate that we had some great Thai board members, but none of them wanted to be heavily involved as had their own lives and businesses to run.

They were more than happy to give us the benefit of their wisdom, particularly in all things Thai, and attend meetings and represent the foundation if needed, but that was as far as it went.

You could never tell what the Thai government would do either. They had already announced that foreign nationals could not hold positions on a Thai board that required official signatures, which meant foreigners could no longer act as president or secretary or treasurer.

What would happen if foreigners were banned altogether from even sitting on a board, in a similar way to which foreigners cannot own land here? If in, say, twenty years' time we had a Thai board which felt very differently to us and decided to close down and hand everything over to the government, what could those who actually ran the organisation do about it?

We had been blessed with some wonderful volunteers and seen them establish foundations in Australia, Canada, the USA and the UK, as well as the original Netherlands charity.

Some of these volunteers had donated their lives to helping us, even though in some cases they had never actually been to Thailand, never mind Soi Dog.

These foundations, however, were set up as legally independent groups to raise funds for the work in Asia, and in some cases provide opportunities for tax savings for donors living in those countries. It also, we felt, gave reassurance to donors that we were what we said we were.

Thailand is known for its scams, and being registered in the countries where the majority of our donors lived would hopefully allay those fears that we were operating some sort of scam.

Sadly, there are many individuals who raise money in Thailand and elsewhere for non-existent causes. These overseas boards had no authority to oversee the actual programmes, though. The funds donated were expressly meant to support the work of Soi Dog Foundation Thailand.

So we decided to establish Soi Dog International Foundation with its own board, which would consist of likeminded people dedicated to ending the stray dog and cat suffering in Asia – and possibly the world in years to come.

The foundation would be established in Switzerland because of its long history of stability, and although no actual physical office existed, it would be the overall governing body and holder of funds. In effect, Soi Dog Thailand, other than funds raised themselves, would need to apply for funding from Soi Dog International. Most of the donations were restricted for use in programmes there already, but it would provide a level of protection if, in the future, a rogue

Thai board did decide to do something stupid.

The international board could at least withhold funds and use them elsewhere. In addition, as our work expanded into other countries, the Thai organisation could not and would not be expected to manage that.

The international foundation would involve the other overseas groups and have close links to the Thai and other potential national boards in Asia in the future.

The mission statement and regulations for Soi Dog International would be drafted with a view to ensuring that the organisation continued to focus on reducing the suffering of the stray dogs and cats of Thailand and beyond.

All our board members would be volunteers. I know some people question the value of volunteers compared with professionals, but Soi Dog was built entirely by volunteers and would not exist without them. Even though today we employ many staff to carry out much of the work on the ground, we also have many volunteers who are there not for financial reward but for love of the animals.

I remember reading somewhere that Noah's Ark was built by volunteers, Titanic by professionals – enough said!

Of course, many of our paid staff, particularly those from overseas, are not working for Soi Dog to get rich. If they are, they are going to be disappointed, but at the same time they are not in the situation that John and I are in – working lives over and a pension to live on. They need to earn money to live on, even though they are working here because of their love for the animals and seeing the difference that we are all making.

Volunteers overseas who put countless hours in to help us without ever seeing first-hand what their efforts are achieving are remarkable people. Although many have been helping us for years, others come and go, which is normal. Sometimes people leave after suddenly finding their lives being taken over by the work and wanting their lives back. In other instances, it's because they feel we are now too big and prefer to work with smaller groups where they feel their efforts will make more of a difference.

I fully understand that people move on, but size should not matter. Stopping supporting us because we are getting bigger is ridiculous. Because we have grown, we now impact more animals' lives than would ever have been possible before, and stopping supporting us means these numbers will reduce. As John often says, a charity can only do as much as the funds it raises. Sadly some people, I assume because they feel they need to justify why they are stopping, do so by attacking either myself or John personally or the organisation. I find this sad. You may not agree with everything we do or like me personally, as for sure I can be difficult, but everything we do is geared around helping as many animals as possible.

The worst thing is discovering staff or volunteers who you trusted actually stealing money from donation boxes or raising funds and keeping the money for themselves. They are taking money not from us but from the animals, and that is unforgivable. Sadly, there are many people around just waiting to take advantage of the generosity of genuine people, and we see a lot of this in the animal welfare world. I have a keen sense of intuition and can generally spot frauds a mile off, but even I have been taken in occasionally, though happily can count those occasions on one hand, and the wonderful, genuine people I have been privileged to meet more than make up for the odd bad apple.

The global stray animal problem is huge and nowhere more so than in Asia. It may seem an overwhelming and impossible problem to solve, but if you don't start somewhere then it will always remain.

We have deliberately tried to not spread ourselves too thinly. Sterilising a few dogs here and there is never going to solve the problem, which is why we have focused on specific areas and do as much as is possible in each one before moving on.

Ideally, we will empower people who can continue to operate an ongoing maintenance programme after we have gone. We are always being asked whether we can start working here or there or provide food for this shelter or that. We do what we can and help many other people and groups, but we must not lose sight of our main focus.

If we see a group or individual making a big difference in their area, then we will try to help them as that is one area less for us to worry about. Providing just food to feed stray dogs by people who are not interested in sterilising them is achieving nothing long term, and although we continue to provide just food to some other shelters, it is not something that I personally agree with.

The attitude to the dogs and cats in Asia is one that is often misunderstood. Whenever people see photos of badly injured dogs or dogs involved in the dog meat trade, our Facebook comments page frequently attracts extreme racist comments describing Asians as cruel and worse.

We remove these comments as soon as we see them, but there is no doubt there is a perception in the West that Asians are cruel when it comes to animals. Anybody working in animal welfare is going to see a lot of cruelty, as I have done here in Thailand. Is it worse here than in my native UK, which is known as a nation of animal-lovers? Ask an RSPCA inspector who spends their life investigating cruelty cases and I am sure you would get a different perspective.

The general attitude to animals is different here, but that is largely because of cultural differences and indeed standard of living. I don't believe that Thai people are any more cruel to animals than any Western race. Cruelty exists everywhere, as does kindness. What is different in Thailand is general attitude. In the West, stray dogs don't exist in most affluent countries in any large numbers. They do in poorer countries, and the persecution and indifference to their suffering exists the same as it does in Asia. Just look at what happens in some of the Eastern European countries.

In Thailand, I think the main issue is that personal beliefs actually end up causing suffering where it is not intended.

John describes the situation as indifference, but I don't even think it is that. It is more acceptance of a situation that you cannot change. If you have little money and use everything you have just to support yourself and your family, then stray dogs everywhere just become a part of the landscape that you know you cannot do anything about.

If just one of the millions of stray dogs in this country appeared on the streets of a town in the UK, it would be such an unusual sight that likely the local RSPCA or police would be inundated with calls, and before long the dog would be picked up. These days it may go to a 'no kill' shelter like the Dogs Trust, but equally if nobody claimed it within ten days it could be euthanised. The Thai people generally have nobody to call, even when they see an animal in appalling condition, and even if it was beyond hope and suffering they would think it wrong to euthanise it. Even in Phuket there are still people who don't know we exist, and this is something we are trying to change.

It is the most frustrating part of our work. I remember John getting a call one Friday night from a Thai man about a dog that had been hit by a car and was lying on a grass verge on the side of Phuket's busiest highway. The man offered to wait and show John exactly where it was, which was great. Only after arriving and finding the dog already dead did it turn out that the dog had been lying there five days, and although thousands of people must have passed it, nobody had thought to report it earlier, when it could at least have been spared days of suffering.

Western tourists are often no better. We do get many who report dogs that actually do not need help and are reported just because they are a stray and, as such, they would report it in their own country. I hate to think how many hours we have wasted going to the aid of a perfectly happy beach dog that would be far from happy were we to remove it and put it in a shelter. At other times, dogs that are clearly in need get ignored.

People often ask me how I cope with seeing so much suffering and cruelty. You do become hardened to it or otherwise would not be able to carry on. It is like nursing. The best nurses have to be tough or would not be able to cope with some of the tragic situations they witness.

Whether it was just a particularly bad day, or the culmination of frustration and anger, one dog did find my breaking point. On the surface it was nothing unusual. The dog-catchers responded to a call about a dog in need of help in a busy tourist area. I was in the clinic when the dog was brought in, and it was covered in cancerous tumours, many of which had burst and were discharging pus. It had clearly been in a state for some time and was a case where the dog was simply beyond help and now suffering.

The vet decided the kindest thing was to put him to sleep. I knelt by him and stroked him gently and whispered to him that I loved him as the life ebbed away. I had seen many worse cases, but it must have been the way he looked at me. Tears started to stream down my face, and when he was gone I simply lost it and stamped into the office, cursing all the people who must have seen the dog in this condition for days and done nothing. Amid the tears, I wrote the words of a poem called, *You Keep on Walking by . . . Why, Why, Why?* which is reproduced at the start of this book.

This is no poetic masterpiece, but it helped me to express the frustration and anger I felt.

Is it cruelty to see a dog suffering on the street and do nothing? I don't think indifference to seeing suffering is cruelty, the same way as ignoring homeless people on the streets is not cruelty. There are those that choose to try to help and those that don't. I do know many poor Thais who give up hours every day to source leftover food and then prepare it and go around feeding hungry stray animals, same as there are people who give up their time to volunteer at homeless shelters.

Is it cruel when a Cambodian or Burmese migrant worker snares a dog and then kills it for meat? It is illegal, though would not be in their own country. It is a difference in attitude. If he inflicts unnecessary suffering on the dog before killing it and is indifferent to the pain he causes, then that is cruelty. The cramming of dogs into crates for transport, indifferent to whether bones are broken or whether they can even breathe, is cruelty; the force feeding by pushing a pipe down the dog's throat and pumping rice into the stomach as the dog screams is cruelty; and beating the dog to death or worse, indifferent to its pain and the stress caused to the others watching, is cruelty. Is going to a restaurant and eating a stew made of dog meat cruel? If a vet does not euthanise a dog and allows it to suffer as a result because of personal beliefs, is that cruelty? I don't pretend to have all the answers and everybody must decide what they can live with and what they can't.

What I do believe is that cruelty exists everywhere, and to accuse Asians generally of being cruel is not only not true but also hypocritical in the extreme. Poorer people generally don't have the luxury of being able to make the same choices we do and will look at all animals generally as a source of food, the same as our predecessors did. There is an old saying – 'If it moves, the Chinese will eat it'. It's very noticeable here that as wealth increases there has been a surge in the pet industry, which no doubt will lead to a change in the way people view dogs and cats, though conversely, with more disposable income, more meat is being eaten.

Equally, among the educated young Asians we are seeing a growing awareness of environmental issues, and it is they who are leading the fight for change in their own countries. There will always be criminals in all continents who will exploit animals if there is money to be made. Thieves will steal people's pet dogs and cats if they can make money from it, the same as poachers will kill endangered species for financial gain.

What we need to do is change the attitude of the consumer so that nobody wants to buy ivory or so-called health products made from wild animals that are being driven to extinction as a result. Nobody needs to eat sharks' fin soup, which is seeing the entire eco-system of our oceans in danger of being damaged beyond repair, and nobody needs to eat what was probably someone's stolen pet.

A big difference here to the West is the way people keep dogs in Asia. In most Western countries, a pet dog has to be controlled, which means it is kept in the confines of the owner's property securely. It is taken out for exercise on a leash and only let off in an area where it is acceptable to let it have a run. Here, in Thailand, that is still unusual, and generally only expensive pedigrees will be kept that way, probably for fear of it being stolen or attacked by other dogs. Pedigree dogs here are more a status symbol. Thai dogs are generally allowed to roam free, and it can be difficult distinguishing between a stray and an owned dog.

To complicate things there are what I call 'community dogs', which are neither one nor the other. People will feed community dogs, and they are liked because they warn of strangers and intruders, but if something goes wrong then nobody accepts responsibility.

Although dog bites are not that common here, when they do occur people generally blame stray dogs. The reality is that genuine strays are frightened of people and will run off if approached. Owned dogs in particular become very territorial and protective of their owner's property, which is a common reason to get a dog. Allowed to roam free, an owned dog will often charge and on occasion bite people who walk past the entrance to their owner's house. Community dogs can also become protective of their areas, barking at people they don't recognise and chasing motorcycles.

To improve things, the government are talking about introducing laws to enforce dog registration and identification. As anybody familiar with the UK dog licensing scheme could tell them, it won't work. The only outcome would be an increase in the number of strays as people refuse to pay a fee or risk getting into trouble if their dog caused an accident or bit somebody.

The plan, apparently, is to build shelters in every community to house the stray dogs. Really? It is one thing to build a shelter, and assuming the local authority could find the funds and have the desire to do that, then of course that is just the start. Who would pay for the food and staff to feed the dogs? Who would sterilise and vaccinate the dogs? Who would provide the inevitable veterinary care as dogs fought over the food? Once the shelter was full, what would happen to all the new strays who would replace the ones removed and soon breed back up to the carrying capacity the local food source allowed? Presumably build another shelter?

One only has to look at what has happened in the past to see that such a policy won't work. The few government-run shelters that do operate here are little more than death camps. Out of sight, out of mind is the general view.

Phuket is one of the wealthiest provinces in Thailand, if not the wealthiest province, and even Phuket authorities cannot run a humane dog shelter. Soi Dog provides the only veterinary care the dogs there get, and it is totally reliant on donations to exist. Outbreaks of disease are common, often resulting in large numbers of dogs dying. The local authorities want a place they can dump unwanted dogs but don't want to have to pay for it. It would be kinder to euthanise them than to put them in such places.

Thailand should learn from other countries. Bhutan, although much smaller, is a good example where lessons have been learned. Like Thailand, it is predominantly Buddhist, and like Thailand it has a stray dog problem.

The authorities in Bhutan decided to do exactly what Thailand are considering now. They would put all the stray dogs into shelters. Of course, they could not catch all the dogs, and local people began to see the conditions in the shelters, which were not good, to put it mildly.

The Bhutanese people were not happy with what was happening, and so the shelters were closed and large scale CNVR introduced as national policy.

Today, numbers are reduced, and the remaining dogs and people are happy. Thailand, of course, is much bigger and therefore has a much bigger problem, but the principle is the same.

# My family and other animals

I have already described how Ginger, Lucky, Dam Dam, and Nid Noi came into our lives. My animals are my babies, and although I was not allowed to have a dog or cat as a child I was now making up for it.

Our first animals all came to us before we even had a shelter, and that included a tiny tabby kitten John found dumped and lying in the grounds of Wat Pah Klok. Its sibling was already dead. She needed bottle-feeding and, of course, could not go back after that. We called her Sabu.

A year later in the same temple, John found an abandoned Siamese-looking kitten with the same markings as Suai, my cat from the UK that had disappeared, and brought it home. Of course we named her Suai.

In 2005, a sixth dog arrived in the form of Tripod. John found him as a puppy at Wat Srisoonthorn, one of the temples where John fed the dogs, and the monk told John some local youths had been using him as a football. He was badly bruised and one front leg was badly broken in several places. We had him operated on and sadly one leg had to be amputated, hence the name. Then we took him to the building in Phuket Town to recover.

He promptly came down with distemper so came to what was now becoming our distemper isolation unit: John's movie room at our house. Thankfully he pulled through and has never left.

Anybody who thinks dogs don't remember bad experiences should see Tripod. When going for walks on the beach if he sees kids playing he will not go past them but takes a big detour to avoid them.

Sadly, we lost Junkie as well that year. Contrary to what I had been warned about, he had thoroughly enjoyed his life in Thailand and was always treated with respect by the younger but bigger dogs which had joined us.

Unfortunately, he was already a good age for a Cavalier and developed severe kidney problems. Clearly suffering, and with no chance of recovery, we took the decision that most pet owners are faced with at some time in their lives.

Back in the UK we had selfishly hung on too long with Max, praying for a miracle that was never going to happen, and having put him through additional days of unnecessary suffering, we were not going to make the same mistake again. Junkie was buried under his favourite spot in the garden and a locket of his fur joined the ashes of those that had gone before in the UK.

Many dogs in particular have come in and out of our house over the years, many for intensive treatment for contagious diseases such as parvo and distemper, and some survived and others did not.

You get attached to sick dogs you are trying to save and many tears have been shed over the years. Many others have come and spent weeks, or in some cases months, waiting to go to new homes overseas.

In the early days it was much harder than it is now to get dogs to the UK. Our very first adoption there was Glory. Glory was one of the dogs John fed at a poor temple in Phuket Town called Wat KuKu.

In those days, our sponsored dogs were all dogs that were at temples John was feeding at. An English lady, coincidentally also called Gill, who was from Hull, sponsored Glory. John had first met Glory as a skinny adolescent covered in mange and sores shortly after the tsunami and had treated her on site. She now looked like a totally different dog.

Glory was always waiting for John at the temple despite the painful injections he was giving her, and in one update to Gill he mentioned that she would make somebody a great pet but sadly it was never likely to happen. Almost immediately Gill replied asking what would be needed to get her to the UK.

Basically a lot, but the process was started, and because dogs could easily disappear from temples, John brought Glory home until she could travel a few months later.

Initially she had to go to France, where she stayed with a lovely English lady who acted as a halfway house, until after six months she could go on to the UK.

John used to visit Glory and Gill on his annual trips to see his family, and again Glory provided clear evidence that dogs don't forget, as she was always excited when John arrived years later.

One of the other dogs who joined us was Milo. Milo was a tsunami survivor from Kao Lak, who was befriended by staff at one of the many human charity offices set up there in the wake of the disaster. Volunteers from overseas would come and go, and responsibility for caring for Milo was passed from one to the next.

Of course, eventually the office was closed, and months later somebody posted a photo of Milo, now thin and hairless, sleeping in front of the door of the former office. It was a tragic sight, and John drove up to find him.

In the meantime, word about Milo spread among the former volunteers who were determined to find him a home. In the end a lovely couple from Manchester, who had volunteered and in that time been carers of Milo, said they would take him.

By this time, although the UK had not yet adopted the EU regulations, we had found a way of legally getting around the UK laws.

After his vaccinations, blood test and three-month wait, Milo could go to any other country in the EU, just as Glory had done. A Dutch vet we knew advised that as far as he was concerned, once a dog had arrived in Holland it was now a Dutch dog and entitled to an EU pet passport, having gone through exactly the same procedure that any Dutch dog would do to enter the UK.

Milo's owners would have to travel to Holland, but after three days and a brand-new EU pet passport could quite legally now take Milo back to the UK.

Since then it has become much simpler as the UK was bound by EU regulations (up until Brexit), though they do not allow people to bring in dogs from anywhere by air as accompanied baggage, only as cargo, which is extremely expensive.

Conversely, authorities only allow dogs in on the ferries or through the Channel Tunnel as accompanied baggage. Please can someone explain the logic of that?

This means that it saves a lot of money for people to take their pets as accompanied baggage to the EU and then drive to the UK. Not the easiest of journeys, and fortunately we have volunteers who will take pets over for them. What will happen after Brexit we have no idea, but clearly it will take years to change all the laws. Hopefully they have more important things to do than change a rule that is working and showing up the stupidity of the previous regulations, when dogs had to spend six months in quarantine whether or not they had evidence of vaccinations and blood tests. Obviously we need to keep rabies out of the UK, but the law was way over the top and resulted in many pets dying unnecessarily in UK boarding kennels.

There are far too many rehomed dogs to name them all, but I must mention Cristy (now renamed Polo), who was adopted by the wonderful Donna Freelove. She had seen the photo of me holding the terrified little hairless dog named after our own Cristy, who found her.

Donna was determined to adopt Cristy and came over to meet her. This not only saw a dog adopted to a wonderful home, but was also the start of a great friendship. We have since been in constant touch, and Donna became the president and driving force of Soi Dog UK. Had we had more time, she would have written this book with me.

Our permanent family was also growing. After Tripod came a smallish Tibetan terrier lookalike who we named Junkie II. He initially came to us when Tris, our gardener, dog walker and general helper with anything else which we no longer had time to do ourselves, brought him to us.

This dog had bad machete cuts on his legs and needed urgent treatment. Apparently his owners, a poor Thai couple, loved him but they lived in a very dangerous neighbourhood for dogs in Bang Tao. The area was all Muslim and Muslim men in particular generally do not tolerate dogs in their area.

After treatment, we agreed it was too dangerous for him to go back as they could not keep him secure in the tin shack they were living in. They did come to visit him, though, and after a few months announced they had moved and asked if they could have him back. We agreed because we could see they loved him and Junkie loved them, and we had to always watch Junkie as he was a sworn cat-hater. Our other dogs were all fine with cats, but not Junkie, as we were to find out when one day Yao left a door open and a kitten I had brought home went into the back garden. We came home to find Yao in tears holding the lifeless body of the kitten. Normally our cats have the run of the house and the front garden and the dogs have the back garden.

Junkie's reunion with his family was to be short-lived, however, as a few months later Tris brought a very traumatised Junkie back to us. Apparently, the husband had found another woman and his wife had hanged herself in the same room where Junkie was. So he was back with us.

It is not uncommon, apparently, for Thai men to take, in effect, second wives, though generally from what I have seen a Thai woman scorned is not to be messed with. Of course, many foreign men, particularly older ones, come to Thailand in search of young Thai wives.

In addition, many marriages don't seem to last long when people move here. We have neighbours on both sides who arrived with their wives, and within months the wives were gone and a Thai girlfriend moved in.

Many people have asked me if I worry about the same thing happening with John, and I would be lying if I said the thought had never crossed my mind. John assures me he loves me and has no interest in Thai girls. He actually can't understand why foreign men lumber themselves with Thai brides when they could go down to Patong any night of the week and spend the night with a different girl every time.

I really don't understand it. Why does a mature, educated and successful man in his sixties or seventies dump his wife, presumably paying a fortune in divorce fees and probably alienating his family, to hook up with a bar girl, who he shares nothing in common with and does not speak the same language.

I have heard about mid-life crises and the male menopause, but do these men really believe that the girl loves them? What do they talk about?

You can see them in bars, and the men talk to one another, and the girls talk to the Thai staff or other wives and girlfriends. For the men it can only be about sex, but then why, as John says, not just settle for a night in Patong?

I don't blame the girls. Most of them come from poor areas of Isaan and are working to support their families. There is little or no social security in Thailand and this is why working girls are not looked down upon.

Landing a wealthy Western husband is like winning the lottery for them. Stories about foreign men buying farms and land for their wives' families are often true. The same applies to girls who marry foreigners and move to their home country.

John had two guys working for him in the UK who had Thai wives they had met when on holiday in Pattaya. The guys were always complaining how the girls were always putting any money they got hold of into a jar and every month would transfer the money back to their families.

If you accept that that is what the relationship is based on, fine, but those guys who think it is based on anything else are in severe need of a reality check.

Note: I am not including here the many foreign/Thai couples who do meet through work and social circles and have very successful marriages, or sadly, in some cases, also get traded in for younger models as their husbands grow older, as has happened with more than one of my Thai friends.

Back to my family. It was growing steadily but surely. Ham was next. He used to live under a taxi rank counter opposite Pen Siri, a guesthouse in Phuket where many volunteers stay. Reggie, who has worked at Soi Dog for many years, was staying there on her first visit as a volunteer. Ham had previously been hit by a car, but had recently had another accident and was struggling to move. Reggie coaxed him out with slices of boiled ham, hence the name. Poor Ham only had one good leg. His front left leg was completely useless and both his back legs had impaired movement. After we amputated the front left leg, we were not going to put him back at the taxi rank and he came home with us. He would always join the others on morning walks to the beach, though tended to stop after a couple of hundred metres and wait for the rest to come back. He was a Bang Kaew, a medium-sized Spitz-type Asian breed and one of only two registered Thai breeds, which have a reputation for being extremely loyal and often aggressive. Ham was certainly loyal, but was the least problem of all our dogs. We never had to put him away if maintenance people needed to come into the garden; he never barked and never got involved in fights. Although John always denies having favourites, if pushed I think Ham would be his number one dog.

Tam looked a bit like a collie and lived at Wat Para. John was always having to take her to Soi Dog for treatment, usually bite wounds as she seemed to be a target for the other dogs. She had a horrible high-pitched bark, and when at the shelter getting treatment she would recognise the sound of John's car and kick off whenever he arrived. One day, after yet another wound had been treated, I decided enough was enough and brought her home.

They say you can take a dog off the street but never take the street out of the dog, and Tam was a good example of this. Her walks on the beach were always spent scavenging for leftovers.

Scooby was a tiny puppy with that short velvety coat many Thai dogs have. He was brought in by a volunteer, who had found him behind a market in Patong. The mother and eight siblings were all dead and had been poisoned. Because Scooby was the runt and very weak, he had been unable to get to the poisoned meat and that had saved his life. Hard to imagine now, but when he first came to the shelter he fitted in the palm of my hand. In need of intensive care, I took him home . . . and you've guessed the rest.

Narak was similar. A sole survivor, she had enormous ears and looked more like a bat-eared fox than a dog. She was to grow into her ears and may go to the UK in the future to be reunited with Donna's Polo, who she used to play with when we were looking after her.

Cats were also arriving. Smokey and Sammy were next, followed by Nemo and Noggin. Smokey and Sammy were kittens that just somehow wormed their way through my defences. Smokey was black with attitude, and to this day caution is needed in handling her. One minute she will be purring her head off as you stroke her, then for no apparent reason she's had enough and sinks her teeth into your hand. She's blue in colour and has grown very big for a Thai cat, weighing around seven kilos. She's quite unlike Smokey, who is very laid back.

Sanuk, my other Birman from the UK, died in tragic circumstances. He would wander around the neighbourhood without a care in the world. Sadly one day the maid of a neighbour who had two black Labradors left the gate open, and as fate would have it, Sanuk was sitting on the pavement outside their house. They attacked her and the first thing we knew was when Yao came running in holding him in her arms. I freaked out; he was still breathing, just, and John drove like a lunatic up to the shelter as it was a Sunday and local vets were all closed.

Unlike in the UK, there is no requirement for vets to have emergency cover. Sadly, we were too late. Sanuk was dead on arrival. I can only describe it as like losing a child.

I blamed myself for bringing them to Thailand and for letting them live freely. John, as usual, had his sensible head on and said all the right things, but they did not help me and I was distraught for days. The reality is we have to accept when we take these animals into our lives that in most cases they are going to die before we do and just have to accept that. Losing one in those circumstances is particularly difficult, and although I know he would not have been happy being confined to the house, I still blame myself.

John was repeatedly saying that enough was enough and that if we were going to bring any more animals in, they should be older ones who had never known a home and could have at least a year or two of a good life.

That was the case with Momma, an old dog who had spent all her life on the streets and had been brought into Soi Dog with a serious injury. We brought her home and she enjoyed the last two years of her life as all dogs should enjoy all their lives – being a member of a family.

Both Narak and Scooby had been puppies, though, and the two latest additions Nemo and Noggin been young kittens, much to John's despair. Following the death of Momma, he said enough is enough and no more puppies or kittens as they could well outlive us.

Nemo was also blue, and I had taken him home to nurse with the inevitable result. He had a badly infected penis as his brother had been suckling on it in the mistaken belief it was his mother's teat. They had been hand-fed at a foster home because their mother had died. Nemo seemed a bit lost on his own so John brought his brother, who we named Noggin, back from Soi Dog. At first they spat at each other, but that only lasted a day and they are now inseparable. Noggin is ginger and white and they look nothing like each other. Noggin sees himself as Nemo's protector and it is lovely to see them curled up with one another.

We had been up to eleven dogs and six cats and in serious danger of being described as hoarders.

As usual, things did not go to plan, and not long after Momma passed away we got a call about a cruelty case in Bangkok we were asked to help with.

Nothing unusual in that, and this was a case of a six-month-old dog that had been attacked by a man with a ceremonial sword. The pup, which lived at the home of a poor lady with his mother and sibling, had been out and spotted the work boots of a neighbour outside the neighbour's door. Having gone to investigate, he began to chew on the toe cap of one of the boots. The furious neighbour chased him off and went round to see the lady, who offered to pay for new boots. That was not enough for the man, though, and later that evening he went again to the lady's house and hacked off the front two legs of the young dog as punishment.

The lady rushed him to a nearby vet, and as news of what had happened got out among local rescuers we were asked if we could help with treatment.

We had him transferred to a specialist vet in Bangkok who could give him the best possible chance of survival. One leg was still attached, just, but was impossible to save so had to be also amputated.

John had to go to Bangkok for a meeting and went to see the dog that, amazingly, was friendly with all the staff, despite what another human had done to him.

What an example dogs can be. I can't imagine many humans being friendly to a species that had cut off their legs.

He told me that the dog had had both legs amputated below the knee and the vet, who also had a degree in engineering, had said that she would try to make prosthetics for him.

Well, you can guess the rest. Here was a dog in the same situation as me, and if anybody understood the issues with wearing prosthetics, it was me. So another young dog was to join us.

Once he got the all clear I flew up to Bangkok to meet Cola, as we had named him, and it was love at first sight.

We were back up to eleven dogs and six cats. As an aside, the man who attacked Cola was arrested and charged under the new animal welfare law. Sadly, his punishment did not fit the crime, and he received only a small fine and a short period of probation. We continue to petition the courts to impose stiffer penalties on those who carry out such cruel acts on animals.

I don't advocate having so many dogs, never mind cats in one family. I actually think two dogs is the ideal number. Why? Because we only have two hands and all dogs love attention, and trying to give eleven dogs attention at the same time when you return home is not easy. Also, trying to control what in effect is a pack of dogs when you take them to the beach can also be a challenge.

We usually take them out very early to hopefully avoid other dog owners. The sight of a pack of dogs charging towards you and your dog, even if they only want to play, can be unnerving to say the least. Nid Noi can be aggressive, and if another dog is spotted we always try to get him on a lead. Dogs are pack animals, and if one behaves aggressively to another dog, the others will follow.

It is the same with cats. Like most Thai dogs, all our dogs are fine with cats; Dam Dam, our small black dog, has been a surrogate mum to more kittens than I care to remember. If one got loose, though, and Junkie, our cat-hater, saw it and chased it, then the others would be sure to follow.

As much as I love them all, if, as Donna suggested, someone wanted to take one of them and give it a really good home, then I would have no problem in letting it go. But that is unlikely to happen, particularly as they get older. I would even let Cola go if I was sure he was going to the right home. Being able to be the sole dog or one of two living in a home has got to be better than being one of ten or more, especially when most of the time your humans are not around.

At times it is easy to forget that other animals besides dogs and cats live on Phuket, although most of the mammals have long since been hunted to extinction for food or sale.

One night we did catch sight of a mongoose in our car headlights, but never before or since. Wild monkeys inhabit the mangroves and some of the wooded hills on the edge of Phuket Town, which local people tend to feed. As the number of dogs reduces, they are getting braver and going into villages bordering the mangroves, breaking into houses and stealing food. Previously dogs would have kept them out.

What there is no shortage of here are birds, reptiles, and insects. It is unusual these days to see large monitor lizards wandering around the area where we live as Thais do eat them. There are some smaller ones living in the lagoon that borders our back garden, and occasionally one will come ashore, but our dogs, particularly Junkie, are on regular patrol, and if one does come ashore it doesn't hang around for long.

The dogs have never caught one, but it keeps them amused, and they always look very pleased with themselves having seen it back to where it belongs.

Same with land turtles and tortoises. If a Thai spots one you can be sure they will stop and pick it up. There is plenty of bird life, including sea eagles and beautiful kingfishers, as well as the many Indian Myna birds that are generally quite tame and will think nothing of walking through open doors into your house. Sometimes their curiousness can be their undoing and although generally too quick for the dogs, we have come across the odd one that probably Junkie has caught.

Small geckos are also very common and live in and outside every house, much to the consternation of our maid, Yao, who has to clean up after them. She is always very pleased with the cats when they catch one. The number of tailless geckos John and I have rescued must number in the hundreds. When threatened, geckos will drop their tail, which continues to wriggle. The theory is that the cat or other predator will go for the tail, allowing the gecko to escape, who will then rapidly grow a new one.

I think our cats are generally wise to this trick, though we do sometimes see one with a new tail growing.

Frogs are also numerous, and during the breeding season can make a real noise. I have learned to shut off the noise and don't even notice it. One of the Laguna staff told us that our next-door neighbour actually put a formal complaint in about the noise. Considering that the land behind, which is empty and marshy and not owned by Laguna, must be home to tens of thousands of them, what exactly he expects them to do I have no idea.

We don't have much trouble with insects and rarely see a spider. You do need to be wary of flying termites, which can rapidly build a nest and enjoy nothing more than eating wood and plasterboard. Like us, most people have their homes treated and regularly inspected to ensure none are there.

The other creature that is plentiful, although you could go years without ever seeing one, are snakes. Ever since our first night in Thailand when we found our two cats from the UK attacking a snake at the house our builder had rented for us, I have been a bit paranoid about snakes. I don't wish them any harm and not all are dangerous. Once or twice I have seen a bright green tree snake that is apparently harmless; at least it is if you are not a small lizard or bird. Cobras are another matter. If we didn't have dogs then the chances are we would probably never see one; even though they come through the garden, they do so quietly and generally at night, and are not looking to meet you.

We did come home one night and when John opened the back door which leads into a store room where I have my freezer, there was a cobra raised in attack mode spitting and growling at him. (Yes, cobras do make a noise).

John immediately closed the door, told me what he had seen, and grabbed a pole and a dustbin lid to act as a shield and reopened the door. The snake had, of course, vanished and we were not about to start peering under the freezer or shelves that were in that room looking for it. The door into the house was also open so it could be anywhere. Snakes can get through very tight spaces.

John decided to open the window in the store room and leave the doors open on the assumption that hopefully the snake, once it was dark and quiet, would leave. I was a bit nervous going to bed that night, I have to say, but at least our bedroom door was close-fitting.

The next day there was a commotion at the side of the house and there was the cobra, being confronted by our dogs. John threw the dustbin lid at it and it literally vanished.

Snakes can move extremely rapidly, and we assume it shot through the railings and next door; cobras can also, like most snakes, climb and swim very well.

On another occasion when John was out walking the dogs, a huge snake came onto the patio. I had a kitten with me who alerted me to it. I literally hurled the kitten through the door and shut it behind us. I watched as the snake, which I believe was some sort of python, or possibly a very big King Cobra, slid around the patio, peering through the windows before disappearing down the garden.

John was sure I was exaggerating about its size, but believe me, this thing was huge. Yao thought it very funny and told me that looking through the windows meant it would be back. It never did come back to my knowledge, I am happy to say.

If I am giving the impression of Thailand as being a dangerous place to live and infested with snakes and vermin then that is not the case at all. If it wasn't for the dogs and their heightened sense of smell and hunting instincts, then I would be able to count on one hand the number of times I had seen a snake.

Now it is not the snakes' fault, but my animals are my babies, and if you have a wild animal that can kill one of your babies around then one of them has to go.

Our dog Ginger was a real snake-hunter and absolutely fearless. She would attack first and think second and had dispatched quite a few snakes in her time. One day, though, when she already had an eye infection, she got it wrong. Although she grabbed and killed the snake, this was not before it had sunk its fangs just above and below her eyes. John immediately took her to the vet and it was a good job he did. Although it was only a few minutes' drive away, she was already collapsing when he arrived there.

Fortunately, Dr Trethep keeps anti-venom, but it was touch and go whether or not Ginger would make it or not, and she was in a coma for three days. Dr Trethep said he had never had to use so many bottles of anti-venom on one dog before.

Ginger survived, but it left her totally blind. It didn't stop her going on walks to the beach or having the odd argument with one of the other dogs, but her snake-hunting days were over. Junkie has now assumed that mantle.

If we get the chance, we will pull the dogs away and lock them up, by which time the snake has usually disappeared. On occasion it doesn't and has clearly made a home for itself under the house or is mortally wounded; then we have little alternative but to kill it as quickly and humanely as possible.

A pair of very long-handled garden shears do that, but you have to be careful, as a cobra can kill a person with its venom if you don't get treatment rapidly. Sometimes we also get cobras at the shelter, and over the years have lost one or two dogs to snake bites.

Sometimes I am asked how we ended up with the animals we did, when we have worked with literally thousands over the years. I can't really answer that question. It was just something at the time. There have been others I would love to have adopted.

Disco, who had been a distemper survivor, used to live outside a dive shop, sleeping, as many Thai dogs, do in the road. One day somebody deliberately drove over him but, amazingly, he survived. He was called Disco as he had these jerky movements caused by nerve damage. He was always happy, though, and would charge to the gate, tail wagging wildly when I went to visit the run he was in.

We were always going to adopt him, but always something happened and another one took his place. Eventually he did come home, but only after he had been diagnosed with terminal cancer and had days to live. At least he had a few days in a real home before we had to say goodbye.

Tess was another of my all-time favourites. She came to us in the very beginning and moved from the dog pound to the new shelter, where she lived for many years in A1.

Sadly, she was not good with other female dogs, and we knew that her and Ginger would forever be fighting so never was adopted. She died very suddenly, and John had a sala (an open pavilion used as a meeting place) erected in her memory in A1 as a Christmas present for me.

As my canine and feline families grew, so did my human family. I had not been back to the UK since my father died ten years previously. My adoptive sister and family came to visit us but stayed one night before moving to a hotel in Patong.

Clearly our lifestyle was of no interest, and I have not seen or spoken with her since. I would make regular duty phone calls to my mother but that was it.

Here in Thailand it was different. Our Burmese and Thai workers looked upon me as something of a mother figure, and I loved them all.

Like kids, they could be naughty from time to time, but we were becoming very much a family in those days. As the foundation got bigger, that tended to get harder to maintain, which is one of the downsides of success.

The big plus, though, is that you can help so many more animals, and nothing beats seeing a dog or cat that you know would never have survived without us getting adopted and going off to a new home.

That again often brings more people into your lives as you get to meet new owners, even if only by email. In addition, more people were coming to Phuket to visit Soi Dog and volunteer. Our entire lives were centred on Soi Dog.

Any thoughts of taking up golf had long gone. John had used to spend half of his time on holidays here scuba-diving. Armed with all his own gear and now living here, he could go whenever he wanted. In reality, he has been out once.

Our plans to visit all of Thailand and the neighbouring countries also had gone out of the window.

In 2014 we had been in Thailand more than ten years, and other than a short shopping break in Kuala Lumpur or Singapore, had not had a proper holiday together in all that time. John had made regular trips to see his mother, sister, and sons each year, but that had stopped since her death.

Karin, John's sister, with whom I also got on great, would come over regularly each year, and his sons had an open invitation.

I had made it clear that I had no wish to return to the UK; just the thought of the flight made me cringe as I knew my stumps would swell, which they did.

I recalled the cold when I had to go over following my father's death, and even though it would be summer, an English summer is still cold to somebody used to thirty-two degrees plus throughout the year.

In my opinion, the UK had also become very much a nanny state – not being able to smoke anywhere was just one example.

But in 2014 John suggested we go back for a visit. Soi Dog in the UK had had a successful reunion in the south of England the previous year, and there were plans to have one in June in Wakefield, which was only a few miles' drive from Leeds, where we used to live.

John seemed to have answers to all my objections, so in the end I reluctantly agreed. We would stay with Karin, and would also have a short trip to London to see a couple of shows. Although I could obviously no longer go fell walking, driving into the Dales would bring back memories.

I would visit my mother, but only if she thought I was there for a short trip, as no way was I going to spend more time with her than duty called for.

In the end, we organised a family reunion with aunts and uncles as well, so other than a visit the following day, I did not have to spend too much time with my mother alone.

I am glad I did it, as meeting up at the reunion with so many dogs that I had known, together with owners who I had previously just conversed with by email, was wonderful.

Seeing dogs such as Glory and Milo and Cristy, that I thought I would never see again, was just wonderful. There were many dogs we had rescued, including some from the Bangkok floods, and many had travelled a long way to be there.

When we went for a drive into the Dales, we went to Grassington, which had been the start and finish point for many of our walks, with Max and Junkie particularly liking the river there.

Even here Soi Dog now had a presence in the shape of Betty, one of my favourite dogs, who now lived right in the centre of the village, her owners being the proprietors of a very popular café that catered for the many tourists who visit there.

We repeated the trips again in 2015 and 2016, only this time the events were held at the side of the River Wye in Ross-on-Wye. A more idyllic spot is hard to imagine and both events were roaring successes, even attracting visitors such as Claudia, who flew over from Switzerland for the event.

In 2016, we also managed a few nights in Cornwall. The singer Will Young, who had become a supporter and visited the shelter in Phuket, had a cottage right on Bodmin Moor and offered us the opportunity to stay there.

As I had never been to Cornwall and John said I would like it, off we went. John was right; it is a lovely county and he took me to Padstow, Land's End, the seal sanctuary, and other tourist sites.

We went to Leeds as well, and as on previous trips, took home suitcases packed with food items not available in Thailand.

The years 2015 and 2016 would see further unexpected and unwelcome medical issues. One morning in 2015, I woke up and, as usual, opened my computer and could not read a thing. It was like I had just lost my vision overnight. I also could not drive as I couldn't see what was straight in front of me. After seeing the eye specialist, I was diagnosed what is known as macular degeneration, a disease normally associated with old age.

Furthermore, one eye had the dry type and was untreatable; the other the wet type, for which there was some treatment that may or may not help.

Fortunately, in my case the treatment worked, but it was my worst nightmare. I am not timid and can put up with pain but hate, absolutely hate, getting water in my eyes.

The procedure involved a nurse repeatedly dropping eye drops into your eye to anaesthetise it. Once numb, the doctor would inject a needle into your iris. It was like the worst possible thing I could imagine, even though it did not hurt, and once I could see again I was not rushing back for check-ups.

Then, in 2016, John was diagnosed with advanced prostate cancer that needed treatment sooner rather than later, and he decided to have it all removed and the surgery done in the UK.

He would have to spend several weeks there and said it was crazy for me to also be there for all that time. He would stay with Karin pre- and post-operation, so we agreed that I would fly in and meet him in London the day before he was to be admitted to the hospital.

I would then travel back with him to Leeds and stay with him until he had to go back for the first check-up and catheter removal. I would then fly back to Thailand and he would return to Leeds when he was passed fit to fly. He would fly out mid-August and surgery was scheduled, subject to getting the OK, for mid-September. This meant I could ensure all the last-minute jobs on the new Soi Dog hospital were completed and still get to the UK when I could be of most help to John.

I had also not been feeling great, but put it down to all the hours and pressure of getting the hospital done.

# Dreams do come true

The new Soi Dog hospital in Phuket was the culmination of a dream that had started back when we came across Naga at the hotel all those years before.

On moving to Thailand, the dream resurfaced with the starting of Soi Dog. Leone, who died in the Boxing Day tsunami, and I had talked about her dream of opening a sanctuary where abandoned puppies could be taken care of.

I dreamed of something even bigger: a sanctuary for all dogs that needed our help and a modern hospital where we could give them the best treatment available.

A fanciful dream maybe, but in 2012 one that was now actually happening. The land was ours and more runs were being built to accommodate the increasing number of dogs coming into our care, including, of course, one especially for abandoned puppies as Leone had dreamed of.

The wonderful Jeanne Marchig Animal Welfare Trust had supplied the funds for a badly needed separate cat hospital. Up to this point, cats were in cages in the same room as dogs, which was stressful for them to put it mildly.

The dogs were either in the small original clinic, which consisted of twelve permanent tiled cages with rusty doors, on top of which were stacked collapsible cages. A hastily built extension on the side served as a quarantine area.

Once the dogs were past the critical stages, they were moved to what we called the C runs, which were a series of large cages, about two metres wide and a few meters long, each housing dogs being treated for various ailments and sorted by whatever they were suffering from.

So all skin cases would be in one run and orthopaedic cases in another and so on. It was overcrowded and in the dry season very hot, and in the rainy season very damp. Not the ideal situation for treating sick animals.

In early 2012, with the floods now gone and the land bought, the dream of a modern veterinary hospital where stray dogs could get the best possible treatment resurfaced in my mind, and I began to formulate plans.

I am no architect or vet so to design what I wanted to be the best vet hospital was going to be a challenge. The logical place to start researching was online, and I began to search for existing animal hospitals and write to organisations in the US and UK in particular.

I visited the best of the existing Thai hospitals in Bangkok and universities to see what type of equipment was available locally and what would have to be imported.

Organisations such as the Dogs Trust put me in touch with suppliers in the UK and suggested other contacts.

Obviously building an animal hospital in Thailand would present challenges, not least because of the climate here.

My emails from 2012 and 2013 are full of conversations with suppliers and 'experts', as well as the initial begging letters to larger organisations asking for support of what would be the most expensive single project Soi Dog had ever taken on.

My philosophy was and always has been that if you are going to do something then do it right or not at all, and I was determined that this would be the best hospital ever.

I filled books of graph paper designing every room down to the smallest detail. My desk was piled high with catalogues from suppliers all over the world.

The Thais are very clever at copying, and if I found exactly what I was looking for in a US catalogue, I would then approach a Thai company to see if they could make the same thing at a lot lower cost. Certain items, though, would have to come from overseas as they were too difficult to copy.

I certainly learned a lot. I'd always thought that ceramic tiles did not absorb liquid and were therefore perfect for hospitals. Not so. Ceramic tiles and the joints between could and would harbour disease and dirt. It was necessary to get vitrified tiles and use special cement and silicone-based grout. These were not easy to find in Thailand at the time, and we ended up buying virtually every such tile available from different suppliers.

It was not made easier by the fact that in their attempts to save money, contractors will cut corners whenever they can, and half the tiles I had to condemn because they had skimped on the special adhesive, which was easily checked by tapping on the wall.

If the tile sounded hollow, there was no adhesive behind. At least half the tiles had to be re-laid, which in the end cost the contractor far more than if he had done the job properly in the first place.

I imagine construction anywhere can be frustrating, but Thailand must be in a league of its own. I learned a lot and could literally write a separate book on the subject.

Corruption is everywhere, including the construction industry, whether paying backhanders for planning permission or architects charging the contractor to be recommended for the job, which in turn leads to the contractor having to make that money back through ripping off the client wherever he can.

The first basic designs were drawn up by the architect based on my sketches in March 2012 and the first detailed plans followed six months later.

In October 2013, twelve months later, I wrote the email below to the architect which is an example of what I was dealing with.

> Dear All,
>
> Myself and Khun Reggie have spent two days going through the 'final' blueprints.
>
> Attached are our findings. There are many pages of mistakes and errors.
>
> We appear if anything to have gone backwards, not forwards.
>
> We are now in October and clearly our meetings have been waste of time as items I thought agreed upon have been removed and items I thought were understood have not been put in.
>
> Water, electricity, flooring and tiles were never discussed and [I] was told would come later. They now appear on the blueprints and have no relation to what we want.
>
> We cannot continue like this. I suggest another meeting as soon as possible. If you cannot do this work please advise so we can find somebody else to complete it. Our own villa plans were completed over the internet in three months without any meetings.
>
> We are now approaching one year since first plans were drawn up and now over three months since the contractor advised [we] could complete in around a month.

It was to be another year, during which I must have aged another ten, before finally work got underway. During this time, I had tried to persuade John and the board to make the hospital two storeys, but John drew the line at that. Looking back, he would agree that I was right as usual, but I did not push it, as my demands for only the best of everything for the dogs had already pushed the budget up by a considerable amount. I did manage to get it made a bit larger, though.

If the nearly three years of planning had been challenging, then overseeing the building itself was if anything even more so.

I have already mentioned the tiles, but you had to watch absolutely everything, and in the end we got rid of the first contractor and brought another in to finish the job.

It was not unusual to come in and find a wall going up where there should not be one, and having been married to a builder I could tell when something was not straight or in the wrong position.

I was on site most days from early morning, not getting home until well after dark.

Weekends I would make up John's meals for the week ahead so all he had to do was take it out of the fridge in most cases, or boil some pasta and heat the sauce up in a microwave.

Fortunately, John loved spaghetti and tomato sauce so that generally took care of two meals.

I would get lunch at the shelter and was usually too tired to be bothered when I got home, so Heinz tomato or mushroom soup out of a tin with some bread was my usual evening meal.

The building phase went on for two years. On Friday evenings we would go to the pub and more often than not I would drink too much, much to John's annoyance.

Eventually, in September 2016, the hospital opened, and despite the budget soaring, the cost was covered by hundreds of donors.

Not everybody agreed with it. Our then animal welfare director told anyone who would listen that it was a white elephant. She had refused to get involved during the planning stage, and now it was finished, I was quick to tell her that if she didn't like something then was her own fault as she had been asked often enough for her input.

As it turned out, even she had to admit it was an amazing facility that offered innumerable opportunities for training. In addition, it now became easier to hire new vets as all of a sudden we had a facility that was a pleasure to work in.

Looking back, there are of course certain things which we would have done differently, the principal one being building two storeys, not one, as the number of patients coming in was already rising, meaning we needed to double up in some areas.

Every detail, though, was taken care of. We even had UV in the air circulation system, which a visitor from the United States told me was now being used in hospitals there; this kills most airborne bacteria, including smells.

You would never guess that there were over 150 dogs there at any time based on the smell – or rather lack of it. Piped soft music played throughout the facility, as tests had shown it helped to relax the dogs.

The hospital would be named the World Dog Alliance Hospital as they, through their wealthy Chinese founder, had donated the required $250,000 for naming rights.

Mr Genlin surprised me by handing me a cheque at a conference he was hosting in Hong Kong. At last we also had an X-ray machine, which meant dogs no longer had to be transported in a back of a truck, often with broken bones, just so we could see what was needed.

Our isolation units were also state-of-the-art with self-contained air circulation systems in negative pressure rooms to ensure that the deadly airborne distemper virus, in particular, could not be spread. Of course, you can have the best systems in the world, but if the staff ignore basic procedures then disease will still spread and that certainly happened.

In the end we had to convert the old clinic to be a distemper isolation unit and the isolation areas in the new hospital became intensive care units.

The additional space was certainly needed, and a new purpose-built isolation unit will be a future project.

Hopefully one day we will see an end to diseases like distemper and parvovirus in Thailand as has occurred in the West, but unfortunately that will be a long time coming with so many stray dogs in the country.

During the final months of construction, I had not been feeling very well, but I hated going to the doctors even if I had time.

I did go and had a tooth abscess seen to before flying over to be with John, who had been diagnosed with advanced prostate cancer.

During the time our hospital was opening in Phuket, John was in the UK preparing for surgery to have his prostate removed. I didn't let on to John, but I was very frightened and indeed angry that this could be the beginning of the end for him. There were so many things we had planned to do together that had not happened.

On arrival in London I found a big lump on my neck, which I guessed was something to do with the tooth abscess.

John's surgeon lanced it for me, but otherwise I felt fine. John had always expected that at some point he would get prostate cancer. He was a big believer in diseases being hereditary, and his father had died of it in his early seventies so he had been monitoring it for some time.

His father was extremely fit and never smoked or drank, other than the odd beer, and did a lot of walking and playing golf. His mother, on the other hand, had smoked like a chimney all her adult life, liked her tipple in the evenings, and lived until nearly ninety.

John was never therefore concerned about smoking. My natural father, on the other hand, had died in his fifties from smoking-related lung cancer.

# The End

Although I was sure it was nothing more than a tooth abscess, that was the first in a string of health-related events that occurred over the next four months culminating in my death.

Not long after John came back from the UK, I got a terrible pain in my left shoulder one evening.

I have a high tolerance to pain, but this was pure agony. John whisked me off to the hospital, where an orthopaedic surgeon examined me, or tried to, as no way was he going to touch my shoulder.

He prescribed some powerful morphine-based painkillers, and thankfully that took the worst of it away, though I was to have a nagging ache for some time afterwards.

Looking back now, this is apparently a classic symptom of lung cancer. In the next incident I literally just went dizzy, and John told me afterwards that I was speaking in what the Bible describes as 'tongues'.

I was talking gibberish and using non-existent words. This lasted some minutes and then I was OK again. John suggested I go straight to the hospital, but I refused. I was fed up with hospitals. I did, though, agree to go for a full check-up and saw a general doctor who had practised in California and was now living in Thailand.

She was really nice and sent me off for various tests, but could not see anything to worry about.

This was in December and she arranged another appointment for me in early January. On this occasion I had a chest X-ray and also saw a blood specialist.

The result was that I was told my X-ray was clear and that they could find nothing wrong with me and I would live for many years yet. That was nice to hear, though I still did not feel great and had a lot of headaches. I would have preferred if they had found something which explained how I was feeling.

John suggested I should have a scan, but the doctor said there was no need and a waste of money. Two weeks later, I was cutting John's hair when I began to feel dizzy again and had to run to the toilet to be sick.

When I returned, John told me I again was talking gibberish just like before and this time he wasn't taking no for an answer.

He called Khun Toom, who recommended a neurologist at the hospital who could see me that afternoon. I went for the appointment and she told me she suspected I had developed epilepsy and began doing tests. Not epilepsy, but she would like to do a brain scan. From the brain scan it was clear now why I was having headaches, the sudden dizziness, and talking gibberish.

My brain was full of small tumours. Well, I had hoped they would find something so would know what was causing me to feel unwell as I wondered if the doctors thought everything was in my imagination. I would have preferred it to be something else, though. She also suspected that these were secondary tumours and wanted me to have a full body scan. Sure enough, this doctor knew what she was talking about. So did the chest doctor, who told us that my previous chest X-ray was not clear at all and said a general doctor may well have missed what he could see.

What the specialist could see, and what the scan confirmed, was a tumour in my right lung, right on the area where oxygen was piped to the brain. They also suspected other tumours in my body and possibly bones.

The chest specialist did not skimp on the truth. 'You probably only have a few weeks to live,' he declared before leaving John and I in the hospital room to digest this news.

We went outside and had a cigarette. 'Now you will be able to do just what you want without having to worry about me,' I quipped.

That did not go down very well with John, of course, and we just sat and cuddled.

'How am I going to be able to live without you?' he asked.

'Don't worry, I am not gone yet!' I replied.

It was decided that I would be flown to Bangkok for specialised radiation treatment on my brain and they would carry out tests to determine possible ongoing treatment.

Where the tumour was in my lungs was not easy to access safely so they could get a biopsy and see exactly what they were dealing with, whereas in Bangkok they had more experienced surgeons.

They also had far more advanced CT scanners. So for the second time in my life, I was transferred by air from Phuket to Bangkok, only this time I was on a regular Thai Airways flight accompanied by a paramedic.

I spent two weeks at the hospital and John stayed at a hotel a short walk away. The radiation treatment was done most days, and together with pain relief, my headaches were easing so it was doing some good. They also did tests and further scans, but getting information from them was not easy.

John sent copies of all the tests to a German oncologist, who one of our supporters had recommended, and he was happy to advise and explain more about what was going on.

John would take me downstairs regularly where I had developed a taste for Starbucks' cheesecake and large hot lattes. Normally, I hate sweet things and prefer tea to coffee, but whether it was a side effect of the treatment I have no idea. I was developing weird food cravings similar to the sort of cravings people associate with pregnant women.

John and I would also go outside regularly to have a cigarette or three, much to the annoyance of the doctors, who were telling me I should stop. John pointed out to them that having been told I only had a few weeks to live, stopping smoking now was not only a bit late but would simply add a lot of stress to me at a time I did not really need it.

As an aside, John did stop smoking shortly after my death – not because of health issues, but because he no longer wanted to enjoy something that had killed me.

I 'celebrated' my fifty-eighth birthday in the hospital. John, bless him, brought me a beautiful bouquet of flowers. He did fly to Korea late one night for an important meeting with a Korean congressman, but was only away for twenty-four hours.

While he was gone, I did manage to fall out of my wheelchair, which did not help John feeling guilty at leaving me at all.

With my radiation treatment completed and tests done, the hospital advised I could return home and made an appointment for me in two weeks' time. The thought of actually going home and spending some time in my own bed and seeing my babies again was wonderful.

The flight back was not pleasant. I had a lot of pain in my legs now as well and was no longer able to walk on my knees to the seat as I had done on other flights. Falling off the very small wheelchair with which they transfer you from seat to aircraft door did not help my mood either, but eventually we got home and I could relax in my own bed.

I was determined to go downstairs and even told John I wanted to go shopping, but he told me no way was I doing that. I could not get my prosthetics on, and getting in and out of the wheelchair was getting harder.

Nurse John got me a commode onto which I could slide so I did not have to crawl to the bathroom. He also scoured Phuket for Twix chocolate bars, which had become my latest ridiculous craving, and cooked me Chinese-style stir-fried vegetables using organic vegetables that Khun Toom sourced from a health food shop.

A friend, whose wife had been diagnosed with breast cancer two years earlier and was told she must have a double mastectomy, had sent up some herbal concoction that she had taken and ended up completely cured, which I was now taking.

Also CBD oil which John had brought back from UK for himself, plus masses of turmeric powder mixed into a paste with natural yoghurt. A disgusting concoction, but again something that had worked for somebody else who had been diagnosed with terminal cancer.

The reality was it was far too late for miracles now. The scans indicated that the cancer had not only spread to my brain, but was also in my kidney, liver, bones, and probably other places too.

I managed a few days at home, which is all I had dreamed of when I was in Bangkok, so although the doctors there must have known I would never make it back to my follow-up appointment and were keen to just get rid of me, they had done me a favour by at least allowing me these few days in my own bed.

I woke up on the fifth day at home with terrible stomach pains and an ambulance was called.

I knew time was running out and had hastily scribbled some instructions to John in the event I did not make it home again.

The doctor there was clearly shocked when John told him about the follow-up appointment as he clearly knew there was no way that I would ever make it.

John was given the choice of me going to ICU and being on an incubator to keep me going a bit longer, or going to a room on a general ward and receiving palliative care.

An awful decision to have to make, but he chose the right one. The lovely neurologist who had first discovered that I was not faking some mysterious illness took over, and with increasing amounts of morphine to combat the pain, I remember very little of the last few days.

John was there throughout the day and at night my maid, Yao, came to sit with me. Khun Toom would also visit, but at my request John told nobody else as I did not want people seeing me like this.

Then one night, John did not go home. I just made it to the thirteenth, our lucky date. The date we chose to get married on. I was struggling to breathe now and having to have a tube put into my lungs to remove liquid almost hourly, which of course was not pleasant. I could no longer speak.

At 1 a.m. I sat bolt upright and John took me in his arms and that was that.

# After Life

Gill died with John by her side on 13 February 2017 at the age of fifty-eight. Since then this date is known by SDF as International Gill Dalley's Remembrance Day, in honour of their co-founder.

Following his wife's death, John Dalley posted a personal tribute on SDF Facebook in which he wrote:

*I apologise for the lack of personal response but have been overwhelmed with condolences which give an indication of the regard with which she was held throughout the world.*

*She died in my arms peacefully after fighting to the end, as always, but this was always one battle too far even for her.*

*I do understand that there are people who would have liked to have said goodbye, but it was Gill's wish that she be remembered as she was and not in her final days.*

*It is absolutely no exaggeration to say that without Gill there would be no Soi Dog today.*

*When she lost her legs in 2004 I was fully prepared to end it then. Gill would have none of it.*

*I well remember her head doctor in Bangkok, who was a Sikh, telling her that none of the medical team understood how she had survived, and he believed she must still have a purpose to fulfil. Gill's response was; 'I do'.*

*The current shelter, cat hospital and most recently the new dog hospital, were all designed and exist because of her, and were all built because of her desire to provide a refuge to animals who had nobody else to turn to.*

*A perfectionist, she was determined that the animals would have the best she could give them. She toiled night and day for three years to design and supervise the building of what is Asia's largest and most modern hospital for dogs.*

*Another doctor back in 2004 told her that double amputees in Thailand rarely wear prosthetics because too difficult and painful to use. He also said to her I think you will be different. Once she had taught herself she told me to get rid of the wheelchair as would never use again.*

*Nobody was aware of the constant pain she suffered from her legs. Most of the time her stumps were covered in blisters and sores owing to the heat and humidity here not suiting the socks and liners amputees have to wear.*

*But she never complained and always refused to use her wheelchair when I tried to persuade her to take a break. It has remained in our storeroom for the past 12 years, and only came out this past month.*

*These are just three of many photos I have of Gill.*

*The first is from January 2005 and taken less than three weeks after she discharged herself from hospital managing a mobile clinic after the tsunami. Prior to that she counselled survivors and relatives of the disaster in Takua Pa and Phuket. She never stopped for 3 months and put off learning to walk again to complete the mission.*

*The second is my favourite, and shows her happy, with just one of the thousands of dogs she was responsible for rescuing and transforming over the years.*

*The third is what drove her. She was always a champion for the underdog whether an animal or a human. This particular dog now lives on the Yorkshire Coast in the UK. One of around 50 a month that SDF now adopts from the shelter that She established.*

*Thank you again for your kind words and thoughts.'*

Following Gill's death, John spent many months reflecting on their life and love together, often sitting quietly and listening to favourite music in the Dalleys' tranquil sala at the end of their garden at home in Phuket, surrounded by the couple's beloved family dogs.

It is here that he faced up to life without his soulmate, finding notes, photographs, and special keepsakes, and recalling memories to share for this book.

In sharing this remarkable story of his wife, John chose to write the final section of this book following Gill's death by continuing to use her own 'voice', which reflects their unique intimacy and understanding of each other.

So now I have gone. Looking back, do I have any regrets? For sure I wish I could have stayed around longer, though I would not have wanted to live without John, so in some ways I am the lucky one to have gone first.

Our lives are full of instances where we would have liked to have turned the clock back and done something differently. I wish I could have met John earlier in our lives, but then who knows if the relationship would have been the same. I like to think it would, as I believe we were destined to be together.

Over the years I had been saving money so that one day I could ask John what his bucket list is and maybe fulfil it, but every time I asked him what he would like to do, or where he wanted to visit most before he died, he just shrugged and said, 'We still have not got around to seeing Thailand yet!'

In relation to the major choices, I have no regrets. I am often asked if I knew then what I know now would I have gone into that field to rescue that dog? The answer is yes and I truly mean that, because I was responsible for the situation and I believe everybody should be responsible for their actions. I could just as easily have died or lost my arms as well, so was lucky to have just lost my legs.

When Donna and I first discussed writing a book I came up with the title Just Gill, because I am nobody special. I have more than my fair share of faults, and when people describe me in some of the ways they have following my death, they really don't know me.

At my funeral, John said that I was his hero. If that is the case then you should have told me when I was alive and often, and not waited until I was dead, JD!

I don't have any regrets about the dogs, other than maybe not digging my heels in and insisting on a two-storey hospital...

Soi Dog was my choice – nobody forced me – and I believe I have made a difference in this world for a lot of animals and prevented a lot of unnecessary suffering.

Some people may say, 'Well they were only stray dogs or cats'. It is precisely because they were only stray dogs and cats that nobody wanted that made me want to help them.

They were the dust of life, and I have no doubt that it is because I was unwanted that I feel so much empathy for them and found it easy to help them.

If I have upset some people along the way then so be it. The animals have always come first, and if you don't like what I do, you know what you can do – and plenty have.

John would always tell me that I have to be more diplomatic and pleasant to people. My answer is always the same – 'If it benefits the dogs I will do it, if it doesn't then I won't.'

I hope John can now find people who feel the same way we did to take over and carry forward the work we started. We, and I mean everybody who has helped us over the years, hopefully have laid some strong foundations on top of which others can build a magnificent structure that will eventually lead to a day when there are no more homeless dogs and cats.

A big challenge, but the basics are now there so no need to start from scratch. In whatever way you look at it, Soi Dog Foundation is a remarkable achievement, of which I like to think I have been a part of. It is probably no exaggeration to say that today it is impacting directly the lives of more animals than any organisation anywhere. It must continue because it is so badly needed.

Before I died, I told John to never forget our secret word and to look for me when he sees or hears it. As I have mentioned, I also left him a note, written in Bangkok, under my pillow, written on the back of a plan I was drawing up for what was now the old clinic. Word for word it says:

> IF IT HAPPENS.
> 1) Plain coffin – Home – Where – up to John. Just plain wooden box or bin bag or cardboard box.
> 2) Morning – Home – People to House – Talking – Music – Glass of wine etc. Celebration of life – not death.
> 3) Lunch
> 4) Burn at temple – not monk service if possible.
> * What I would like if possible.

I wrote on the other side when I was back home, and before my final journey to hospital:

> HOME
> 'My eternal Love'
> Know I'll always be
> with you John
> XXX

Bless him, he did that and also played the music I wanted, although being John he drew the line at playing Queen's 'Fat Bottomed Girls' at my funeral, and instead played more appropriate songs when they carried me away to the crematorium.

Thankfully, 'Fat Bottomed Girls' and similar music I loved was played at my wake. I wanted people to celebrate my life, not mourn my passing. It was lovely to see all the staff driving in the sparkling clean Soi Dog trucks and me in the back of one on the journey from our house to the temple. Bless them, the police even gave us an escort and stopped the traffic. I could have done with that on more than one occasion when I was alive, not now I was dead.

At the end of the day, my life became 'all about the dogs', and John, of course. I hope you have enjoyed reading about it. If not, blame John! Goodnight.

# Epilogue by John Dalley (January 2019)

Gill was both an ordinary person and an extraordinary one. Many people see beyond their own four walls and know that there is much that is wrong in this world of ours.

As the lady who wrote to me after Gill's death said, 'The number [of people] who actually try to do something about it are relatively few in number, and those who inspire others to do the same rarer still.'

Gill was very much one of those few. What made her extraordinary in my opinion, and the bravest person I ever met, was the way she overcame a huge setback and refused to be beaten.

That sums Gill up: somebody who would never be beaten. She was stubborn as a mule and there was nothing she wouldn't do to help the abused and neglected. I have seen people, including vets, cringe as she would soothe and cuddle a frightened dog despite it being covered in fleas and lice that would rapidly jump onto her.

I have also seen them cringe as she ranted at them for not doing what they should have done to help an animal.

In relation to Soi Dog, her motto was 'It's all about the animals', and she tried to drill that into everybody who came to work or volunteer. When she saw someone who clearly was not doing that and thought the animals came second to their own ambitions then a collision was inevitable, and there would be only one winner.

There is no doubt that her stubbornness and refusal to let herself be beaten enabled her to carry on when most other people would have at best taken a back-row seat.

Once she had taught herself to walk again, she told me to put her wheelchair in the attic as she would never use it again. Other than the odd time her legs needed some repairing, or in the last month of her life, she never did use it again. She did use wheelchairs at airports, as she learned that meant she got whisked through immigration queues.

What people didn't see was the severe pain she would often put herself through to not use the wheelchair. Thailand's climate, with its high humidity and high temperatures, is not best suited to wearing artificial legs which require silicone liners and woollen socks to ensure a tight fit. It was rare that she did not have painful ulcers on her stumps, and I would often hear her cry out as she pulled off her legs at night, often removing a layer of skin as she did so.

I would often suggest she use her wheelchair for a bit, but she would just glare at me as she slapped plasters over the wounds and pushed the prosthetics on again next morning. The only way you could tell she was in pain was if she was not walking quite as well as usual.

Most people who didn't know her had no idea she was a double amputee. Her gait was not normal, but if you did not know her would assume she had a hip problem or similar. She was an amazing dancer, and even after losing her legs could dance most people off the floor, including most definitely me!

She was certainly not perfect and at times could be very difficult to live with, but although it might sound clichéd, she was my hero, my lover, and my best friend, and life will never be the same without her.

People tell me that in grieving it generally gets better after two years, and you just remember the good times. The truth is, of course, that everybody is different.

The first three months after Gill's death I guess I was in shock, and by taking care of all the legal issues was able to focus on that. Since then the loss has only multiplied, and I genuinely do miss her more each day.

We are now starting to approach the second anniversary of her death and the loss I feel does not lessen with time but grows. I look for her everywhere; our maid tells me she sometimes smells her perfume, but I think she just says that for my benefit. Sometimes I do hear unexpected sounds in the bedroom at night and sit up and call her, but of course she isn't there.

Gill did believe in some sort of spirit world and I wish I did, but the rational person I am tells me that death is the end.

Some people have said you will meet somebody else, even if just for companionship. The reality is that Gill has made it impossible for me to have another relationship; I was blessed to be an ordinary man who had the good fortune to be married to the most extraordinary woman. Even just companionship would not work; I would be a terrible companion. I love my wife and always will. I spend time with her, even though she is not here, reliving memories and places we used to love, and it would not be fair to impose that on somebody else.

Am I lonely? Yes, but only because I am missing my soulmate. I could go out and socialise with people if I chose to, but find myself doing that less and less.

Back in the UK, I revisit some of the places most dear to us. Walking up Ingleborough, our favourite peak (and no easy trek these days for me) early on a beautiful morning with not another soul to be seen brings wonderful memories flooding back, and whether she can hear me or not, I give her a running commentary of the walks.

I stop in on the way back at the Junction Inn in Otley, where we would always call in on our way home from days out in the Dales or lakes with the dogs. Thankfully, just like the Dales, it has not changed at all and still has probably the same water bowls on the floor for its canine customers. Here, we would sit and discuss how to save the dogs of Thailand when we retired there. If you are ever in the area go and have a pint of Timothy Taylor's Landlord (the best pint in Yorkshire Gill claims), and picture Gill and I with our two dogs plotting the future for dogs in Phuket.

In York, also on Stonegate, is the pub called the Punchbowl (I assure you we were not alcoholics!). Walk through to the back room and it is little changed from the night when we first looked at each other as more than just friends. We would return there on anniversaries and also Christmas Eve as the area has a real Victorian Christmas feel to it.

We always intended to continue our weekly day in when we moved to Thailand just as we did in the UK. Unfortunately, the demands of Soi Dog meant we never had a spare day, and despite promising that we would find one, never did.

Today, every Sunday after taking the dogs out and answering any urgent emails, I have resurrected those days in, and nothing will come in the way of them if I can help it.

At the moment I spend some time writing this book before retiring to the *sala* at the end of the garden, surrounded by the dogs, and listen to music we loved, which of course brings memories flooding back.

Some make me smile, some make me cry. It could be love songs I would sing to her as we drove out for a walk all those years ago, or musicals which we loved and shared together.

I will drink a few beers, and when it gets dark, we'll go inside and settle down and I watch home videos of our life together before Thailand, or one of our favourite films, or an episode of James Herriott's TV series *All Creatures Great and Small*. Those days are both happy and sad, but the dogs certainly enjoy them.

People ask if our own animals still miss her. A strange question maybe, but for sure they still look for her. I still use her car sometimes, the car which meant so much to her as it was modified so she could maintain her independence, and I cannot bear to let it go.

When I do use it and come home, the dogs hear it and rush round to the gate excitedly; I guess they are hoping it is her, as they don't do it when I use my truck.

Similarly, unless somebody asks if they can have something, as a good friend who rescued dogs in Bangkok did with a few pairs of Gill's trousers, her wardrobes are the same as when she left. I don't see why people throw everything out. There are no charity shops here, and why have empty wardrobes? People say it helps in moving on. Does having an empty wardrobe help you move on? I prefer to leave things as they were.

I do, of course, continue to work to help the dogs, but without my partner it is not the same. Some people may be shocked by that statement, but Gill and I were a team, and half a team can never be as effective. We were total opposites, but complemented one another when it came to helping animals.

We had already determined that to ensure Soi Dog lived on after we were gone, we needed to focus on finding people who were as determined as us to continue to help dogs. I have no idea how long I have left, but despite the doctors thinking they had got it all, my cancer has spread and I have been told it is now terminal.

What that means who knows? I saw an interview once with the wonderful broadcaster and author Clive James, who died in November 2019 after losing his battle with leukaemia some ten years after he had been told it was terminal. I am having treatment that I'm told could halt the spread for years.

One thing I do know is that I have no fear at all of dying, other than ensuring my animals will all be taken care of and knowing that Soi Dog is in safe hands. That is now coming to pass, and I can gradually step back and let others younger than I and with more energy take over and take Soi Dogs to even greater heights until one day, hopefully, it will no longer be needed.

Soi Dog has some wonderful people who are there, whether in Thailand or elsewhere, because they love dogs, and I hope have seen the impact it has. Every year since the foundation began it has helped more and more animals, and although I shall never see it, I dream of the day when there are no more unwanted dogs anywhere because of what Soi Dog achieves in the future.

Gill said shortly before her death that she would not be one of those people that went to her grave saying 'if only'. Unfortunately, I am not in the same boat. My own childhood left me finding it very difficult to share feelings. As Gill would say, I built walls around myself to ensure I did not get hurt. I do regret not telling her when I had the chance what she meant to me and not telling her that every day. That is all she really ever wanted or needed and I did not give it to her. Wouldn't it be wonderful if we could turn the clock back? But we can't.

*Just Gill* was what you wanted to call the book and I have followed your wishes, but you were far from 'Just Gill', my darling – you were someone very,

very special who I was extremely privileged and lucky to have spent at least a part of my life with.

I commissioned a statue of Gill by the renowned Italian sculptor Albano Poli to be placed in the sanctuary garden where she would often sit at her computer. No donations have been used to pay for it, and no doubt Gill would be appalled at my spending money on such a thing. I am sure many people will think it an odd thing to do.

Would they think it odd if I bought a new car or travelled around the world? Gill had been saving money for me to fill a bucket list at the end of my life, but there is nothing I want or nowhere I want to go without her next to me; I would just be regretting she was not there. This statue will enable people to actually see the person whose determination built the place where they are now standing, and hopefully they may look upon it and say, 'Well, if just Gill could do this, what can I do?'

I suppose it is my own personal Taj Mahal. Not the same grandeur, of course, but my tribute to the love of my life, and if people think it is a strange thing to do that's their problem not mine.

At the time of writing (early 2019) the statue has arrived at Soi Dog from Italy, fifteen months after work started, and is to be installed and unveiled to coincide with what would have been Gill's sixtieth birthday (not something she would have been celebrating!).

Special thanks to Donna and Claudia for their input and coming to Verona towards the latter stages, and especially Paola for the introduction to Albano Poli, who at over eighty years of age is still a great artist and sculptor and ensuring everything has gone well.

The legacy Gill has left is really quite staggering. Success sadly often breeds envy, and there are plenty of people who resent and are jealous of the success of Soi Dog and claim it has grown too big.

The reason it has been so successful is because of literally the blood, sweat, tears, and sheer hard work on the part of Gill and others to make it so. Because of its success, Soi Dog has done more for stray dogs and cats in Thailand than probably all other organisations combined. Gill would applaud anybody trying to help animals and support if she could, providing they were focusing on the animals and not themselves.

Animal welfare has sadly attracted more than its fair share of people exploiting others for their own ends, and it is very difficult to tell the genuine from the fake at times.

One thing is very clear, however – when it comes to the genuine article then Gill was exactly that. As she would say about herself – 'What you see is what you get, and if you don't like what you see, no problem.'

People like Leonard, Alan, Sarah, Donna, Claudia, John Higgs, Janis, and too many more to mention provided the means for Gill to get to work doing what she was best at – not that she was averse to squeezing donations from everybody she herself met.

Gill was first and foremost hands-on. Whether it was setting up and running mobile teams, cleaning dog runs, or designing and building an amazing hospital, Gill was good at whatever she turned her hand to because she was never afraid of hard work and wanted to be the best at what she did, whether it was being the best bank clerk she could be, the finest cook, or creating a dog and cat welfare charity.

Today, many of our staff and volunteers have moved here to help take Soi Dog to the next level. Gill left a wonderful legacy and I'm sure you will ensure it continues to grow.

# Conversations with Gill by Donna Freelove

I wanted you, the reader, to know who Gill was as a friend and a woman. Those who did not get to meet her know of her outstanding achievements in the world of animal rescue, as it is all well documented what she and John strove towards, right up until her premature passing.

John has written in this book about their lives and work together, and here I'm hoping to be able to give you my perspective as a friend.

It's common to speak of people who have passed as if they were perfect in every way and perhaps rightly so. Maybe any foibles or disagreements should pale into insignificance once that person has left us and perspective should take precedence, considering what was really important.

To me, it's far healthier to celebrate the positives of someone's life, based on what they have achieved to make the world a better place and what they have meant to you as a person.

It is extremely easy for me to talk about the positives with Gill, as quite simply she made my life and my world a better place.

It's indisputable: she made the world a better place.

Not to say that she didn't infuriate me at times as I did her. But I can only ever remember throwing my hands up in the air at this incredible woman's habit of, at times, of suffering fools gladly, giving the benefit of the doubt to the Nth degree and sometimes being almost apologetic to folks who took advantage of her extraordinary kind nature.

Of course, none of these are bad traits at all, if anything, she had the most endearing qualities that we should all strive for, however, seeing a friend get hurt as a consequence of those wonderful qualities could be a hard pill to swallow.

That is it, in a nutshell. Gill Dalley had a better, kinder, more tolerant nature than anyone else I know and having her as a friend taught me things that I will always try to practise yet never master as she did.

If Gill had been just any other Gill, not the animal-rescuing legend that she was, and to me still is, (Christ, she would positively wince at the word 'legend'), I wholeheartedly believe that she would still have made my life and world a better place just for knowing her.

Fact is, in my life there have been so few completely selfless and totally giving people. Gill was totally giving of herself, of her heart, and cared about you in a way that we should all care about ourselves.

As mentioned in the foreword of this book, Gill and I had commenced writing notes for her life story to be called *Just Gill*. I have to say how incredibly hard it was to even get Gill to talk for even fifteen minutes exclusively about herself. We would sit down in her outdoor office, which leads onto the Dalleys' garden, dogs vying for attention, kettle constantly on the go providing us with mugs of Yorkshire Tea, and the ashtray getting fuller by the second as we attempted to start this damn book. Gill's trusty laptop would be open, phone next to her on the table, 'ping, ping, ping' with emails popping through, which she would be eyeing up as we spoke, with her orange reading glasses perched on the end of her nose. She would reply to emails as we spoke sometimes, not even missing a beat of the conversation which we were simultaneously having. Invariably, she would only be a minimum of ten minutes into talking about her life before she turned the conversation around to mine.

Some of my most humble memories of Gill, which I can still see in my mind's eye, were watching her eyes light up with happiness when I was talking to her about the love I received from my parents and grandparents growing up.

Of course, the conversation at that time was meant to be about her childhood. Hers, as John has written, was not a childhood that anyone would wish on any child to experience – a child, like all, who did not ask to be born into this world.

To sum it up, she was unwanted, rejected, and pretty much unloved compared to what most of us are fortunate enough to have experienced.

She would tell it as if she was talking about another person, showing no self-pity, no bitterness or malice at those who had treated her this way. It saddened me that she talked as if this was 'normal', like she had not been even unlucky in any way.

What truly humbled me once was that I was so shocked at some of the things she told me that I welled up with tears. I tried to hide this as no way did I want her to feel my pity. It wasn't even pity; it was just me hurting that such a wonderful human being hadn't really experienced the love and security that all children should receive.

Gill, being Gill, perceptive as she was, noticed my sorrow. She asked me why I found it upsetting. I remember saying to her, 'Gill, you talk about this as if it is normal,' and she simply said, 'Well, it is to me'.

She told me that nobody should cry for her, then explained that she was glad that it was her who had experienced the harshness because she felt that it was her 'lot in life' and she had been 'lucky' enough to have found her own coping mechanisms to deal with rejection that a less strong person may not have.

The fact that these 'coping mechanisms' included bulimia, I guess, shocked me even more. The one 'salvation' she had found to eliminate her pain at her comparatively loveless early life and to help her control her grief at the loss of her adoptive father, who was her only dear love prior to John, was in fact a very damaging crutch that she thought got her through her darkest hours.

In her words, there were times when she wanted to feel numb, to take control and power over her own body as she didn't feel that she had control over the things that had emotionally hurt her, so she ate, then she purged, and before she could even analyse what was happening a self-destructive cycle of bulimia had begun.

To me, it seemed so hard to understand as Gill was such a beautiful-looking woman, and photographs of her early years also showed her as being extremely attractive, but she explained to me that rejection had made her feel ugly, made her feel that she deserved to be rejected and unloved, and the only way she could erase this ugliness and control the hurt was to go through this ritual.

She started in her late teens by eating nothing in the day and then binging on food late in the evening. Gill would then, in her mind, correct this by using laxatives. For some years she never even considered throwing up until she saw a film where a young girl did this, so that made the process easier for her.

It was her coping mechanism, resulting in being not so much about the food or what she thought was her ugliness and unworthiness, but more about her first feeling of control over her emotions.

So we would sway from heart-wrenching bombshells like bulimia to her then asking me to relay stories about my childhood; her eyes would well up with sheer joy when I talked about my family holidays and the loving, secure, warm family times.

She would ask about my love and relationship I have with my mum, like she had a thirst for wanting to hear how normal, healthy mother/daughter relationships grew into friendships with age.

She always had the knack of showing more interest in you and your life than of her own. She would ask about my dad and would well up with tears about him dying, like it somehow never crossed her mind that she never even got to meet her own natural father or hold him, yet here she was grieving for someone else's loss.

This was her essence: to feel more for others than she did for herself, to rejoice in their happiness and grieve with them at their own heartbreak. Never did she consider her own losses and the fact that, conversely, her own early life had been, by most people's standards, a tragedy.

Typical of this, I can remember a lady called Lucy coming up to me at one of our Soi Dog reunions in the UK. She came to say hello to me and told me how humbled she was that she had just met Gill Dalley.

This lady told me, 'I have been so excited to come and meet the lovely Soi Dogs and to meet the people involved. I never in my wildest dreams thought that Gill and John Dalley would be here in the UK. I've been a long-time follower and admirer of the Dalleys and almost felt like a teenager in awe when I saw Gill working on the merchandise stand. I thought to myself that this is a once in a lifetime chance for me to tell Gill in person how greatly I admire her for all she has done for the dogs and cats in Asia.

'I waited until I saw the queue die down at the stand and approached Gill. I cannot even remember what I said as I almost fell apart with emotion telling her what a brave lady she was. Gill came and put her arms around me, looked into my eyes, and asked me what was troubling me – she told me that she saw deep sadness in my eyes and asked could she be of help to me. Before I even realised, I was telling Gill that my father had died the previous week and I had almost not been able to attend this reunion. That I had needed to be strong for my mother and family so had not begun to grieve myself. Gill held me tightly and actually cried with me for the loss of my father. She cried for me, someone who she had never even met before and for my father. I felt that, at that moment, I was safe, that I was strong and not alone. What an amazing woman she is.'

I like to think that Lucy will be reading this now and smiling. What she witnessed of Gill's essence that day was real and typical of Gill. She had an insight, a perception of how others were feeling and empathy for others that she always held of much higher importance than her own feelings.

Forgive me if I trip from story to story. We only get once chance here of writing Gill's story, and I dearly want the readers to hear not only what a perceptive, warm woman she was, but how hilariously funny she was without even realising it.

Gill loved Whitby in Yorkshire. When the Dalleys were in the UK, Gill and I rented a beautiful holiday cottage near the town centre while John went down to London on Soi Dog business.

Gill, me, and my Soi Dog Polo checked in, threw our bags upstairs, and opened a bottle of Prosecco to settle in for the night catching up. We could hear a faint beeping noise now and again that wasn't really an issue; we assumed there was an alarm clock intermittently beeping either upstairs or even next door.

As the night progressed and maybe another bottle had been drunk, the noise started to get louder and quite irritating. I was ignoring it, but Gill was concerned that it would affect Polo's ears, as although it was only going off say every fifteen minutes, it was beginning to sound shriller.

We decided to investigate, but it was really hard to ascertain where the noise was coming from. We eventually narrowed it down to a smoke alarm in the dining room, thinking that the battery was dying.

The ceilings in this Victorian house were very high and I'm extremely short. The only way to get to this smoke alarm was for me to place a chair on top of the dining room table and stand on it. Even doing this, I could not reach up properly to unscrew the alarm and remove the battery. I tried and tried but it would not unscrew.

The noise got ever more shrilling and more frequent. Polo was showing signs of distress now and sloped behind the settee for sanctuary. Knowing that Polo was unhappy spurred Gill into action. I was getting nowhere and she was on the warpath to kill this pesky noise.

She stomped into the kitchen, rifled noisily through the drawers, and stomped back into the dining room armed with her chosen weapon of destruction. I was ordered down from the chair. To my horror, she said, 'I'm going up there.' Of course, I told her she couldn't, but 'defeat' just wasn't in Gill's vocabulary.

Bearing in mind that Gill was on two prosthetic legs, she launched herself onto the table, then onto the chair, and attacked the smoke alarm with a fish slice until it smashed off the ceiling. Still unable to open it, she placed it in the backyard and we agreed to leave a note and a tenner for the owners of the cottage to compensate for their damaged smoke alarm.

The third bottle of Prosecco was opened strictly by way of celebration. Polo returned to the party and we continued our night.

Beep, beep, beep. It began again, even louder. Gill leapt into action, stormed through the dining room, through the kitchen to approach the yard . . . on her way through the kitchen she noticed a red light flashing on the slightly opened dishwasher door . . . beep, beep, beep!

I can't talk about Whitby without adding a tip Gill taught me there – always to pop a silver teaspoon into an unfinished bottle of Prosecco to stop it going flat overnight. I still wince when I see people throw unfinished Prosecco away at the end of a party and know what Gill would say about such waste.

While in Whitby, we would talk until the cows came home. I loved to wind Gill up. For a woman who had had such an amazingly interesting life, she did, in a very lovely way, have a very naïve innocence about her. She was very shockable, and when we, as friends do, talked about teenage experiences, her eyes would widen up at tales of some escapades that many would take in their stride.

She would tell me about her love of shoes and how the only thing she liked about herself in her early days was her slim, long legs. She loved to buy and admire shoes, and spoke of how for many years after she lost her legs she would still spot a great pair of shoes, say at a function, almost go to ask the lady wearing them where she bought them, and then remember that sadly she wouldn't be able to wear them on her prosthetics. She would talk about how she loved to style her hair in her younger days, that her legs and hair were her favourite features; she also told me that after her accident she developed some allergies, including a severe reaction to hair colourants, so sadly could not colour her hair any more.

As we get older, particularly women, it is great to be able to hide the grey with hair dyes. It's an option that we maybe take for granted and it really hit home to me, the sadness of the other ramifications her accident caused. Gill didn't particularly dwell on these things but talked about them casually as if they were just 'her lot'.

While in Whitby, we would go to one of Gill's favourite restaurants – the renowned Magpie Café – where she would always have crab salad and Prosecco. Gill was a pescatarian; she would eat fish but not meat. She explained that she would only eat something that she would be prepared to catch, kill, and prepare herself. Gill would stock up on fresh fish and cold-water prawns, which she would freeze, wrap in newspaper, and take back to Thailand, where I'm told the package would still be frozen on arrival.

Whitby is made up of steep hills. When walking back out of the town and up to the cottage, Gill, because of her prosthetics, would have to build up great momentum and storm forwards to be able to walk uphill. Once she'd started walking, she had to continue or would almost fall backwards; often this would mean that she could bump into people if they suddenly got in her way, but she would still have to surge ahead, hearing them mutter 'rude woman' or similar, not realising her situation or that she couldn't stop to apologise.

I guess these are the things that we don't consider that people go through. It's pretty hard to use the word 'disabled' with regard to Gill, as even the loss of both legs didn't actually disable her.

As disability was hardly acknowledged in Thailand, it was a surprise when Tesco's in Phuket added a few disability parking bays close to the door of the shop. Gill used to drive there for supplies shortly after the bays were introduced. The car park attendants took their job very seriously and when Gill pulled up in her car, she had hardly turned the engine off before both attendants approached to tell her that these sacred bays were not for her. She simply lifted her trouser legs to the two amazed and nervously smiling men who had obviously seen her at the shop many times before but never realised.

In the UK, we have a system whereby disabled people are issued with a special key to gain entrance to disabled toilets. Not being a UK resident, Gill didn't have one of these keys but still needed the extra space to manoeuvre herself in a cubicle . Once while in the UK, she asked a toilet attendant whether she could give her access to the disabled toilet. The attendant told Gill that this was not possible, as in no way did she appear to be disabled. Gill lifted her trouser legs to show her prosthetics. She told me that she did this to open the eyes of the attendant that all disabilities are not visible and in the hope that in future the lady treated others with more respect. Again, typically, this wasn't about Gill, it was thinking ahead to others that may be in her situation.

Despite the horrific pain and sores that Gill endured daily, she insisted on wearing her prosthetics in public, and woe betide anyone who suggested that they would get her a chair to sit on. Often at events I could see how tired she was looking and suggest sitting for a while. Out of the question!

She was there to represent the organisation and to spend time working and thanking people, not to be sitting down.

Gill's prematurely aching bones were another reason to leave the UK, and the chronic rheumatic-type pains she had endured were greatly improved once she lived in Thailand. Whenever Gill was back in Britain, whatever the weather, she positively grimaced with cold and wore as many layers as she could manage.

When we stayed in our cottage, all windows and doors needed to be closed, central heating blasting out, and she would sit huddled up in her faux leopard-print coat, ciggie in one hand, glass in the other, grumbling about the unbearable cold.

Of course she shouldn't have even been smoking indoors as this has been branded unacceptable practice for decades in the UK, but to Gill, this was just another symptom of the 'nanny state' that we were becoming here.

As much as everyone loved Gill and marvelled at how admirably she coped with the loss of her legs, I don't really think that many could possibly realise how difficult the logistics of travelling were for her. The house that the Dalleys had built for their retirement in Phuket has a beautiful bathroom with walk-in double shower. One can only imagine the excitement and planning that went into what was to be the newlyweds' forever home. Sadly, after Gill's accident, that beautiful bathroom was of no use, as of course, it wasn't designed for disability. Likewise, when Gill was in the UK, it was impossible for her to shower normally as facilities aren't designed to take her loss of legs into account. Similarly, the pool at the Dalleys' house stood unused by the couple and was joked about as the biggest dog water bowl in the world.

It is such an honour for me being entrusted with adopting my Soi Dog Polo. When Polo was first rescued in 2013, she was in a dreadful state – so much so that Gill took her home to nurse personally.

When Polo came to me in the UK in December 2013, there were some heart-wrenching photos of Gill at Phuket Airport saying goodbye to her. As flying is so uncomfortable for someone with prosthetics, Gill thought that she would never see Polo again.

The problem with flying is that, naturally, particularly long haul, we tend to swell up with the air pressure of the cabin. Gill would keep her prosthetics on while flying as she would never have been able to reattach them again after landing, so the swelling and pressure on her legs would have been agonising encased in prosthetics for the two flights needed to get to the UK.

Polo arrived in England on the Saturday night. I collected her from Harwich Port, and thankfully she seemed to recognise me as I'd spent time with her at the Dalleys' house while she was recuperating. Needless to say, she'd only been home with me for a matter of hours before Gill phoned to see how she was; she wasn't panicking, but she just wanted to know that she was safe and settled.

We emailed daily regarding Polo's new life. Her health went up and down and Gill was so very supportive, giving me the just the best skin care advice – tips that I now pass onto anyone who has a dog with severe mange and damaged immune systems.

Our Soi Dog UK annual Fun Day was being held in Wakefield six months after Polo's arrival here. Gill and John were coming over for it and everyone was looking forward to seeing them.

Polo was suffering recurring skin infections resulting in MRSA in her paws. It was touch and go with the possibility of her losing one of her paws at one stage as the vets couldn't find a treatment that she wasn't resistant to. Fortunately, they grew cultures and finally found an antibiotic that would help her.

As the fun day was getting closer and Polo started to respond to her new antibiotics, I wrote to John in confidence asking if he thought it would be dangerous for Gill to be around Polo, as if Gill's immune system was weak from her infection, was it worth the risk of her handling a dog who was getting over such a bad infection?

John replied that he thought it would be OK and that the infection Gill had had was quite unique and waterborne.

The fun day was on a large field at a cricket club. I parked at the far side and walked Polo across the field; all this time I could see Gill in the distance standing with her arms wide open waiting for Polo. When we reached her she sat on the ground with her head buried in Polo's back, cuddling her. There were many tears shed as people saw this little reunion between the two of them and the photos of that moment are very precious.

Gill took me to one side that day and gave me a telling off. John had obviously mentioned my concerns. 'What on earth possessed you to even think I would care if I caught anything from Polo?' she asked. I should have known!

It is common in Thailand on the streets at night and on the beaches to see people selling an array of bracelets and wooden gifts. Among what they sell are little wooden frogs with ridges down their backs; they come with a little stick that, when you rub it down the frogs back, sounds like the constant chirruping of insects that you hear in any tropical country.

I bought one of these for Polo before she left the UK and used to play it for her to remind her of home. Her health was always up and down and I hoped it comforted her when she was feeling particularly poorly or irritated by her skin conditions.

Two years after adopting Polo, I moved house and mentioned to Gill that Polo's wooden frog had got lost in the move. Later that year I was in Phuket and sitting having a meal on the beach outside Phen's restaurant with Gill, John, and maybe twenty others. Annabelle and Dennis and some other old friends were with us, and the drinks were flowing. We were laughing and having a fab night and talking mostly about the new posts we were doing on Facebook, bringing the dogs and cats and alive by creating funny characters for them on their journeys to the UK.

Gill was at the end of the table and disappeared at some stage. I assumed that she had gone to use the bathroom, then when she didn't reappear after twenty minutes or so I guessed that she would be chatting somewhere.

About an hour later, I saw this figure in the distance striding up the beach. It looked like the way Gill walked, but I couldn't for the life of me think why it would be her. As this figure got closer, I realised that it definitely was Gill. She presented me with a wooden frog to take home to Polo. Despite the difficulty walking on sand wearing two prosthetics, this amazing woman had walked right down the beach to find a beach seller just so I could take this wooden frog home to Polo.

There were times over the years when Gill and I, like all friends do, would disagree on things – never fall out, but disagree. She was always the first to admit if she was wrong and apologise if she genuinely thought that she had offended anyone.

There were times when people took advantage of her naivety and good nature. Perhaps not coming from a competitive corporate background, she didn't seem to possess some of the cynicism that would have made her question things more. She genuinely took most on face value and believed that all had the same level of integrity as her.

To this end, Gill has been very emotionally hurt over the years when people that she trusted have been disloyal to Soi Dog Foundation in any way. To those who thought that she was confident and untouchable, I would say that I've never seen any other person get so emotionally affected at anything that would cause disruption to the foundation, to the point of making her ill and so very hurt. 'How could anyone do this to the animals?' Not 'How could anyone betray me?'. . . Always the effect on the organisation first and foremost.

There were times when Gill had a feeling about a person, a 'chill down the back of her spine' when she instinctively knew that they were not a good person, or not there for the right reasons. She was very right on most occasions, and I know that at times she wished that she had followed her gut instincts more.

This sixth sense extended to Gill randomly texting if she thought you were having a bad day or may need her. Spookily, she was often right.

I can remember Gill reading a draft of an email to me that she had written to a Welsh female singer, someone who she had met and who had offered to help SDF. She hadn't sent the email yet but had attached a recent photograph of a Vietnamese child whose parents had cooked her pet dog. The child was on the floor crying with the cooked dog next to her. It was horrific and as she was asking my advice at the time about sending the singer it, I said that it was just too shocking a picture to send. Even though I'd previously seen the picture on social media, I just thought it was too graphic to send to someone who perhaps couldn't deal with such images.

I asked whether Gill thought that she had become desensitised over the years, but she explained that she just couldn't understand why everyone shouldn't see the horror that was going on, and until they did then what chance did these animals have?

I didn't attach that particular image to the email in the end but, years later, I do see Gill's point that there is little to be gained from tiptoeing around the facts. The singer never helped us anyway so who knows what the right thing to do was .

Over the years, the Dalleys have had their critics. Sadly, it would seem that the more you put into this world, the more you open yourself up to criticism. Animal rescue seems to attract a wealth of people who think that they could do it better, and instead of rolling up their sleeves and doing so, they sit at a keyboard and attack others.

Social media allows an element of people to build their part up and gain credibility without even leaving their lounge, it seems, and Soi Dog Foundation, like every other organisation, has its fair share of knockers. I've always admired how much decorum both Gill and John have always showed at such behaviour, rising above it and cracking on with the job in hand rather than retaliating to some of the nonsensical things that people comment on within public forums.

Likewise, people like myself who are involved also get criticised often and, typically, Gill's nature was always to care more and hurt more about negativity levied at us as volunteers than herself, as she was fiercely loyal to all around her. I don't for one moment think that every criticism of SDF didn't cut through Gill like a knife and cause her emotional pain in private, but the dignity she always showed is something we all should aspire to.

Gill's loyalty extended to the animals in her care. She would be wide-eyed at hearing of adopters of Soi Dogs taking DNA tests to ascertain what 'breeds' of dogs they had adopted. She loved the street dogs of Thailand so very much that she was almost offended that anyone would need to know what breeds they were made up of.

Her views on the new 'breeds' such as Cockapoos were bluntly funny: 'They're a mixed breed so therefore a mongrel! People are paying hundreds for a mixed breed with a newly invented name when we have a shelter full.'

Gill laughed easily at things and was actually very funny herself without knowing it. I received an email from her once in a different font and colour than normal and replied asking, 'What's with the colour and jazzy writing?'

'To appear windswept and interesting,' she replied. From there started a rally of emails back and forth from both of us that would start, for example, 'Times Roman in Azure Blue to appear windswept and interesting'. This rally continued for weeks until we had exhausted all fonts and colours available.

Her love of Thailand but dismay at not being able to acquire Heinz mushroom soup, thus having to take tins back from the UK in her suitcase, was funny; her stockpiling of Yorkshire Tea and Lurpak butter from Makro I also found amusing, as are her set of Lurpak butter knives that she took with her when she moved to Thailand.

Despite the dogs being adopted to homes in the UK, I think it's a great mark of respect and admiration that Gill was still considered to be the 'mother of them all' and that these precious souls are all in our custody. In fact, we are all looking after them for Gill and woe betide anyone who didn't treat them like gold dust.

Gill often made threats to 'haunt us all; if anything ever happened to her and if the Soi Dog Foundation wasn't looked after as it should be! Another 'Gill-ism' that seemed so far-fetched and impossible at the time.

If I had to pick a favourite memory it would be of our SDF fun day the summer before Gill passed. One of our adopters performed an ABBA tribute show in the evening. When they started to sing 'Fernando', they dragged John up to the stage as their 'Fernando' and he was mortified.

If I need cheering up I watch the video of the night, as I can hear Gill's laughter in the background. It's inconceivable to think that this was only months before she left us, but the sound of her sheer joy at watching John on the stage dressed as Fernando always makes me happy.

Gill had no regrets about leaving the UK. In fact, despite everything, post-meeting JD she had very few regrets in life at all. Of course there were things she may have done differently, but I have to say that her relationship with JD was enviable, even if they didn't realise it themselves. To an outsider, they had both won the jackpot in the love and compatibility stakes, and it was a joy to watch them bounce off each other while working and socialising. BB's and Peppers Bar in Phuket on a Friday night would be a regular jaunt where John would always be deep in conversation with someone while Gill's infectious laughter could be heard above everything. It made me laugh when Gill's beer bottle became dangerously low and she'd call over to John 'Red Alert' to signal the 'emergency' in hand.

Gill's only regret regarding their life together was that they had not been able to find the time to do more as a couple and fulfil their bucket list, but I very much doubt if she had her time again that she would have done it much differently.

Fact is that the SDF – well, the needs of the dogs and cats – would have come first and foremost for both of them, above any bucket list trip for sure.

When Gill had her accident it was touch and go whether she would lose one or both legs. Apparently when she came round after amputation and went into shock on the news that they had needed to remove both legs, JD did not deal with it very well and basically told her that she would just have to cope with it.

When she told me this account, she said that it was something she could never forgive him for. I'm quite straight talking, particularly with folk like Gill, who were the same, and I fought JD's corner as I knew that he too would have been deeply traumatised at his wife nearly dying.

However, Gill wasn't having any of it! 'No, it was unforgivable, when I needed him the most.'

I said to her that she must have forgiven him to a degree or she wouldn't still be so madly in love with the guy. To this, Gill pushed her glasses to the end of her nose, winked, and said 'Yes, and may God forgive me, but everyone needs to keep hold of a trump card up their sleeve, Donna.'

Since Gill passed, I've had many soul-searching conversations with JD. He has been so hard on himself thinking that he never showed her enough, told her enough, held her enough. The reality is, Gill, like many people, but even more so than most, was very insecure and always would have been. He could have held her morning, noon and night but she would have still been unsure of herself.

She wasn't broken but she was emotionally damaged far before she ever met John. She wasn't insecure about her marriage, she was insecure about herself, and that started at such an early age, I doubt her circle of self-doubt could have ever been broken.

It wasn't John's role to fix her – that was beyond his scope. I t was his vow to love her, which he more than fulfilled and will continue to do so forever. Whatever he thinks he failed to do, whatever sort of husband he thinks he was to her, he was the man she loved and wanted by her side forever, her eternal love. She loved who he was and would be so, so proud of how he has managed to even breathe without her, never mind functioning for his own animals and SDF, despite having to go through cancer treatment himself.

On paper, it shouldn't have worked at all. Studious public schoolboy, at times geeky, to whom shows of emotion didn't come naturally, versus emotionally charged, tactile, vivacious yet insecure, somewhat lost soul, but it worked wonderfully. They got through more together than most relationships would have survived and achieved so much. There was still huge passion between them, despite the roller-coaster moments, they laughed a lot together and John noticeably, always, always, called her 'darling' in front of others.

This always made me smile as she would positively preen at the word. I hope that one day John will learn to be as proud of himself as she always was, and still would be, or maybe is, if she could see him now.

There are many funny stories about Gill I could recount which still make me laugh.

I loved the fact that in the UK, when talking among ourselves, we often referred to the SDF shelter as 'the Mothership' due to Gill's presence. It was hilarious when Gill was due to visit the UK, how many Soi Dogs were put on diets beforehand as she would make no bones about telling the adopter that the dog was fat so its life expectancy would be shortened. As soon as Gill felt around the dog's ribcage, you knew you were in for a 'fat dog' lecture.

When John was diagnosed with advanced prostate cancer and being treated in London, Gill arrived and stayed in a hotel nearby to the hospital. We spoke on the phone in the evenings after visiting times and she was very down, terrified of losing him. I know she wasn't feeling well herself and it wasn't helping being holed up alone in a grubby London hotel 'in a room the size of a matchbox and having to walk three miles to have a ciggie.'

Gill would swing from being totally a hundred percent sure that her JD was going to be absolutely fine, no question, to being beside herself with the fear of losing him. I wanted to drive down just to be there for her, but Gill being Gill, she wouldn't have a fuss.

I remember her calling when I was walking on the beach near my home with Polo. She wavered on the phone, almost fell apart but not quite, then quickly composed herself, told herself off for being silly, and then lectured me about keeping Polo's paws dry or her fungal infection would come back!

I recall giving actor Peter Egan (who is a great ambassador for animals and friend of the Dalleys) a call when I returned home from that walk. I just wanted to reach out to someone in London that night, and as soon as I told Peter that John was in hospital, he contacted Gill and if memory serves me correctly visited JD in the hospital the next day.

Again, this was just another example of the people who have huge respect and admiration for what Gill and John have achieved.

Soon after, John's surgeon was very confident that he had removed the affected area and that he would be okay.

Of course, Gill said she 'knew this all along', but what a terrifying time it had been, not only worrying about JD's health but wondering how on earth Gill could have survived without her love if the worst had come to the worst.

Fact is, she couldn't have lived without him. Not even for the animals. She wouldn't have wanted to see another day without JD.

At the time of John's surgery, I thought a lot about what would happen if we lost him.

It would have been a case of losing both of them in one fell swoop. I'd seen and, to some extent was still dealing with, the same degree of grief with Mum losing my dad, and I knew how devastating it would be.

I knew that, like with my mum, when you love someone so completely there is nothing and nobody that can lift you from that pit of despair.

Of course the added complication was Gill living in Thailand; there was no way that she would have come back to live in the UK, and being heartbroken and alone, she would have absolutely self-destructed.

The thought was heartbreaking and I'm sure I wasn't the only one whose thoughts were running away with themselves at the time. I can distinctly remember thinking that as much as I knew how lucky they were to have found their soulmates, the reality was that one day, one of them was going to lose the other.

As much as I love Gill, I just could not have borne to watch her lose John, for as much as they needed each other, John would be the one more likely to at least exist, for want of a better word . . . eventually.

When John told me Gill's diagnosis and timescales, the last thing he said was that 'Gill knows everything'.

Of course she did; she just wasn't the sort of woman who couldn't have full knowledge of what was happening to her.

She rang me within hours and the first thing she said was, 'I don't care what they are saying, I'm not going anywhere as I have far too much to do. Anyway, how's your back?'

Incredible. I was told not to be upset or afraid, that she would always be there no matter what the hospital said. She was going to fight this.

My last email from Gill was on 12 January. It said: 'Love you so much, Gill xxx'.

If I've read that one last written sentence once, I've read it a billion times. Spoken words go into thin air. These written words are my most precious possession and reading them makes me feel so lucky and so loved.

We Skyped a few times when she was able to from hospital before her illness really took hold in the last days. I said to her that I bet she was finding it hard without a ciggy and she told me that she was being wheeled outside for a smoke when needed.

On the last few nights of her life I stayed up through the night and had John at the other end of Skype. I wanted to be with him in some way, with them both until the end, until he messaged to say she had passed while he was holding her.

She had managed to tell him that she loved him and this made me so happy as I knew it would have meant so much and she would have fought through her pain, confusion, and medication to be able to tell him one last time.

When I moved from Warwickshire to Yorkshire, Gill was delighted. I wanted Polo to live at the beach because one of her allergies appeared to be associated with grass, so the sand would surely give her a better quality of life.

Not many people have heard of Hornsea, but Gill told me that one of her few precious childhood memories was of her beloved adoptive dad taking her to Hornsea Pottery on a day trip.

I arrived at the Dalleys' house a few days after Gill passed. Arriving in Thailand made everything even more shockingly real . . . she was gone. Her casket was in the lounge, cigarettes, ashtray, and mug of Yorkshire Tea sat at the end of the casket just as she would have wanted. We removed these things out of respect when the monks came to the house to chant but back they went afterwards.

I went up to my bedroom to freshen up, numb with grief. The first thing I did was to open the patio doors to step onto the balcony to have a cigarette. There on the table in front of me was an upturned small bowl with writing on the base – 'With Love From Hornsea Pottery'. I had never seen this at Gill's house before and neither had John when I asked him. I wonder at the fact that this was very probably a souvenir that Gill and her dad had purchased on their day trip all those years ago and that she treasured that memory so much that she took it all the way to Thailand with her when they emigrated. I'm not at all spiritual like Gill was, but this certainly gave me just the warmest feeling ever under the circumstances, as if it had been placed there purposely to help me get through. Like she knew I'd head for the door to go outside for a cigarette to compose myself so had left some sort of sign to comfort me. Who knows?

I treasure our emails, photographs, her laughter in my head, and her arms around me. I wear her paw necklace all the time and have her keyring attached to my bag. The keyring was sent to her by an American supporter who I hope is reading this. It has a picture of my Polo (then called Cristy) engraved onto it and Gill always had it attached to her handbag.

I also wanted to mention Khun Yao, the Dalleys' housekeeper. Yao was the lady who worked as a maid at the hotel where Gill and John used to stay on holiday and where they got married. She became the housemaid at the Dalleys and was treated more like a family member.

Thai people show emotion quite differently to Westerners. For instance, Yao would never show or talk to John about how devastated she was at the passing of Gill.

A unique Thai trait is almost to smile when sad or nervous, possibly a sign of being non-confrontational.

Thai people don't deal with disability as we do in westernised countries. It tends to be hidden away, and disabled people are kept within the home, not encouraged to lead normal lives.

Gill took it upon herself to start talking to schoolchildren about disability in a bid to raise awareness that it shouldn't be hidden away and that disabled people can sometimes live relatively normal lives.

As is the nature of Thais, there were times when the children she spoke to laughed or smiled nervously at Gill's prosthetic legs when she showed them to the children. She laughed with them to show that there was nothing to be frightened or ashamed of. Gill also visited hospitals to encourage people who had lost a limb that there was life after amputation. One particular patient she spoke about was a young European man whose bedside she sat by after he had lost an arm during a holiday accident

When she was talking to him, he had no idea that Gill herself was a double amputee, and after several visits, during which time he got upset, he told Gill that while he appreciated her visiting him, she couldn't begin to understand how he was feeling.

At that point she showed him what had happened to her and he was shocked as he hadn't even noticed.

After Gill passed, when Yao greeted me at the house with usual hugs, it hit me that she didn't seem as upset as I had expected her to be. She was busy making tea and bustling around the house as normal.

I sat outside cuddling the dogs and Yao bought me (another) cup of tea. I asked her how she was and she welled up with tears she'd been holding back. I took her hand to show her that it was OK to cry, but she led me to the bottom of the garden where we sat out of view of the house and she broke her heart.

In broken English she told me how it was not respectful for her to show emotion in front of 'Khun John'. All I could do was try to convey how much Gill thought the world of her and how invaluable she had always been looking after Gill and their dogs and cats.

It struck me that in spite of how many times Yao would have seen Gill display emotion, she would still never dream of doing the same, despite the very sad circumstances. It also struck me how different, culturally, we all are in some respects.

John and I managed to speak at Gill's funeral. I don't really know how, autopilot perhaps. The huge turnout was so befitting of a woman who had contributed so much. After the service, the wake was held at Peppers, one of Gill's favourite bars. Then John and I went back to the wat to complete the traditional Buddhist ceremony of collecting her ashes. I don't know what either of us were expecting but it was so very different to western cremations.

It's unnecessary for me to go into details but this culminated in me clutching a muslin bag with my friend into my chest back to John's car. John drove us back to the house and we placed her upstairs on her dressing table next to Ginger, one of her beloved dog's ashes.

It really doesn't get more final than that.

John, Claudia and I went to Verona to see the finishing stages of Gill's statue that now stands at the shelter. In the initial stages of the statue being made, Paola would send photographs from the artist showing the progress.

The first editions didn't capture Gill as closely as the finished product. It was hard to tell what was missing but once we had suggested that they perch Gill's glasses on the top of her head, tuck her hair more softly behind her ears and add her rings onto her wedding finger, these subtle changes made such a difference. Most of the time, Gill wore Crocs on her prosthetic feet. For the statue to look authentic, it really had to include her trademark Crocs. The artists that created Gill's statue did not know what Crocs were so we stood and watched him sculpting a pair of Crocs from a picture of a Croc printed from Google.

A big light turned off in my world the moment we lost Gill. It's easier to cope with from 6500 miles away, to pretend that she's still there, and there are still a few seconds every morning when I awake wondering if she has emailed me during the night.

I never see a bag of her favourite sweets – apple sours or salted caramels – without instinctively wanting to buy them and send them to her.

I think of the time that she drove me to the shelter blasting out Meatloaf's 'Bat Out Of Hell' and we had to sit in the car outside the old clinic while she sang at the top of her voice until the song finished.

I think of her when I hear one of her favourite tunes, 'Last Night Of The

World' from *Miss Saigon*, and whenever I think of her a line from the Charles Aznavour's song from the seventies 'She' resounds through my head . . . 'Me, I'll take her laughter and her tears and make them all my souvenirs.'

When John and I attempted to sort some of Gill's belongings after the funeral, we selected a few of her precious things that we knew would be well used and treasured. Her crystals went to UK volunteer Julie Reed, who practises reiki, and these are still used with love and fond memories. Her tarot cards and onyx pendulum cross went to UK adopter Pauline Hall, her watch to long-time friend and SDF adopter Claudia in Switzerland and her leopard print scarf plus one of her Lurpak butter knives to UK adopter Gaynor Lee, who Gill adored for her northern humour.

Me, I'll take Gill's laughter and her tears and make them all my souvenirs ...

I consider myself so very lucky to still have a massive part of her in my Polo, who she nursed back to life. I am luckier than most to have loved and been loved by this amazing woman, who has had such a positive impact on my life.

Gill showed me what unconditional friendship, loyalty and love was, and to feel that from someone who has given so much to this world against all odds is the most precious gift I could wish for in one lifetime.

# SDF: Happy endings
## Examples of the thousands of case studies Soi Dog has treated over the years

## Cheeky

Cheeky was only about a year old when she arrived at Phuket's Soi Dog shelter in shocking condition. Sadly, homeless animals in such pitiful condition are an all-too common occurrence on the streets of Thailand.

On arrival at the shelter, Cheeky was diagnosed with chronic mange. She was depressed and weak, with all her fur having fallen out and her frail body covered in painful, weeping sores.

Fast forward a few years and Cheeky is now living a happy life in Canada after being adopted by Chantal in New Brunswick.

## Leo

Leo arrived at the Soi Dog shelter with shocking injuries. His jaw was broken in two places and he couldn't close his mouth, which meant he was unable to eat or drink. In addition, one of his eyes was protruding from its socket and it was too late to save it.

Nobody knows how Leo sustained his injuries, but vets believe it's likely he was hit by a motorbike or other vehicle.

Although he suffered a great deal as a result of the trauma he endured, Leo's story has a happy ending. He was adopted by Mary-Ann in Ohio, USA, and now enjoys life in a loving forever home.

## Louis

The circumstances in which Louis (formerly Bowie) arrived at Phuket's Soi Dog shelter were horrific. Someone had poured boiling oil over him, leaving him with severe burns. Louis needed months of treatment, and in the first few days, it was touch and go as to if he would survive. He was weak and depressed and not eating, but then, by some miracle, he turned a corner.

Today, Louis lives happily in England, after being adopted by Caroline in Hampshire.

He is a world away from the horrors he endured after being dumped on the unforgiving streets of Thailand.

## Thumbelina

Little Thumbelina (formerly Angel) arrived at Phuket's Soi Dog shelter after being hit by a car. Tragically, it turned out that she was blind, although it wasn't clear if this was a result of the accident or a contributing factor. She had also suffered very serious trauma to her head and jaw and was struggling to walk.

Thumbelina needed surgery to repair her fractured jaw and also underwent treatment for cat flu. It took months of treatment and care for this special girl to recover, but once she did, she found the most wonderful home.

Thumbelina was adopted by Raquel in California, USA, a very special lady who had previously adopted a dog (Feisty Faline, previously known as Roongtiya) from Soi Dog.

Raquel says that Thumbelina and Feisty Faline are now 'best siblings', who love each other very much, with blind Thumbelina relying on her doggy friend to be her eyes.

## Feisty Faline

Feisty Faline also arrived at the Soi Dog shelter after being hit by a car. This is a very common occurrence in Thailand, a country where millions of dogs and cats roam freely.

The accident left Feisty Faline with serious injuries, with her leg and hip badly crushed. She was unable to use her hind legs so hopped like a rabbit.

She underwent surgery at the Soi Dog hospital (a femoral head osteotomy) and had pins and a plate inserted in her leg. She now walks better, but will always have a very unique gait. Feisty Faline now lives with her cat friend Thumbelina (also adopted from Soi Dog) in sunny California, after being adopted by Raquel, who describes her as 'the apple of my eye'.

## Proud

Proud was dumped on the busy highway outside the government dog pound in Phuket. Confused and desperately trying to find her owner, she was running in and out of traffic when she was hit by a speeding car. The husband of a Soi Dog staff member happened to be driving by moments later when he witnessed all the other cars driving around poor Proud as she lay severely injured in the middle of the highway. Parking his car in the middle of the road, he stopped the traffic and scooped her up, rushing her to the Soi Dog shelter.

Proud was bleeding profusely. She had sustained serious injuries to her head and eyes, and for a time, it looked like she would lose an eye. She had a long road to recovery but beautiful Proud made it. Today, she has a wonderful life in England, having been adopted by Kirsty in Warwickshire, who describes her as 'the greatest, most lovable little dog'.

# Cheeky

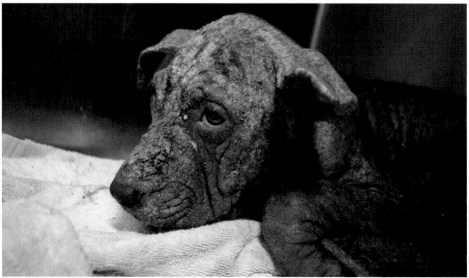

Cheeky on arrival

Cheeky happy and much healthier

# Leo

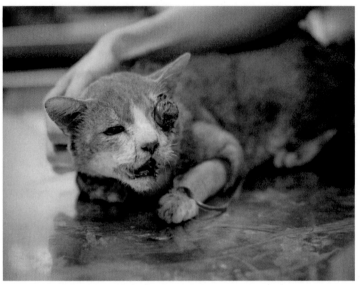

Leo on Arrival

Leo at home

# Louis

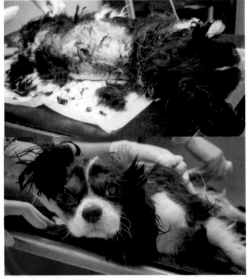

Louis on arrival

Few weeks after arrival

Louis happy and at home

# Thumbelina & Feisty Faline

Thumbelina on
arrival

Feisty Faline at
shelter

Thumbelina and Feisty Faline happy and
posing at home

# Proud

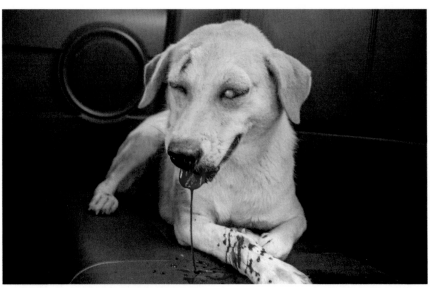

Proud on arrival

Proud happy at Woofmas

# Soi Dog Foundation facts and figures for 2019 (unless otherwise specified)

- STERILISATIONS  119,542 (389,204 SINCE FOUNDED)
- ANIMALS ADMITTED  AT SOI DOG HOSPITALS  4,4,736
- NUMBER OF ANIMALS IN OUR CARE END OF DECEMBER 2019 1,166
- ANIMALS TREATED OFFSITE BY COMMUNITY OUTREACH TEAMS 4,137
- NUMBER OF VISITORS TO THE GILL DALLEY SANCTUARY 5,556
- NUMBER OF VOLUNTEERS AT THE SANCTUARY  881
- ANIMALS ADOPTED 944
- CALLS RECEIVED BY HELPLINE 17,868
- ASSESSMENTS CARRIED OUT BY BEHAVIOUR TEAM 566
- CHILDREN TAUGHT IN EDUCATION PROGRAMME 7,368
- REGULAR DONORS AS OF END OF DECEMBER 32,101
- EMPLOYEES AS OF END OF DECEMBER 2019 279

# Awards to date

2005 (Soi Dog Foundation) – Elizabeth Lewyt Award for work in aftermath of Asian tsunami

2008 (Gill) – Asian of the Year, Channel News Asia. (First non-Asian by birth to receive this).

2011 (Gill) – First Asia Pacific Canine Hero Award (Presented at Asia for Animals Conference, Chengdu, China.)

2011 (Gill and John) – Jeanne Marchig Award in recognition of their Outstanding Services to Animal Welfare over many years.

2017 (Gill and John) – Humane Society International Extraordinary Achievement Award in Animal Protection.

2017 (Soi Dog Foundation) – Charity Film Awards – People's Choice for best film based on Gill and Cola.

2018 (Soi Dog Foundation) – Pet Philanthropy Circle. People's Choice Award Animal Welfare Organisation of the Year.

2018 (Soi Dog Foundation) Pet Philanthropy Circle . Rescue Organisation of the Year.

2019 (Soi Dog Foundation) Ministry of Agriculture Thailand. In recognition of services towards elimination of rabies in Thailand.

2019 (Soi Dog Foundation) Charity Film Awards – Runner-up Best Film.

Just Gill

# Acknowledgments
## John Dalley & Donna Freelove

We have acknowledged many organisations and the *Soi Dog Foundation* global family in other parts of this biography. But we also want to thank those people who made the process of turning our love toward Gill's life and legacy into the beautiful book you have in your hands, so that when memories begin to fade, we can always go back to its pages to refresh them.

What has characterised the whole process has been the enthusiasm shown by the people in charge of producing the book. We approached Victorina Press to publish it because Consuelo Rivera-Fuentes and her partner Lynda Birke are part of the Soi Dog UK 'family' as they have volunteered with us here in the UK, at the shelter in Phuket, and of course, are adopters of Soi Dog *I Nam*. So, our thanks go to the professional team at Victorina Press (Jorge Vasquez, Sophie Lloyd-Owen and Consuelo) who have given Soi Dog supporters the chance to know a bit more of Gill's life and hear it from the top dog's mouth, so to speak. We would also like to thank Fiona Zechmeister, the cover illustrator, who seems to have no limits to her patience. Any changes have been met with a virtual smile and a 'no problem' attitude.

Thanks to the editor, Katherine Trail, for the clarity of her copyediting and for her constant communication with us. She respected Gill's voice throughout and did not attempt to correct any of the grammar or spelling of her notes.
We are very grateful to Jo Hockenhull and Lynda Birke for insightful comments on the first draft of the manuscript. This set the wheels of the process in motion. Thanks also to Barbara Young for her ongoing encouragement and suggestions. Finally, many thanks to you, the readers who bought this book. We hope that you agree with us in that Gill Dalley was not JUST Gill. She was an extraordinary woman full of love for life and animals, and we will always be grateful to her for touching our lives in such a way.

Your legacy will go on forever, dear Gill.